Albert Schmitz
Edith Schmitz

Englisch Aufbaukurs Technik

Handbuch mit Schlüssel
zu den Übungen

Max Hueber Verlag

Übersicht über das Gesamtlehrwerk

Englisch – Grundkurs Technik
2181

Handbuch mit Schlüssel zu den
Übungen   2.2181

Arbeitsbuch   6.2181

Compact-Cassetten mit Aufnahmen
der Lektionstexte   5.2181

Schallplatten mit Aufnahmen der
Lektionstexte   3.2181

Tonbänder mit Aufnahmen der
Lektionstexte, mit und ohne
Nachsprechpausen   4.2181

Sprechübungen   7.2181

Lernwörterbuch   8.2181

Lektürehefte

Zusätzliche Tests

Englisch – Aufbaukurs Technik
2189

Handbuch mit Schlüssel zu den
Übungen   2.2189

Arbeitsbuch   6.2189
(In Vorbereitung)

Compact-Cassetten mit Aufnahmen der Lektionstexte   5.2189

Schallplatten mit Aufnahmen der
Lektionstexte   3.2189

Tonbänder mit Aufnahmen der
Lektionstexte, mit und ohne
Nachsprechpausen   4.2189

Lernwörterbuch   8.2189
(In Vorbereitung)

Lektürehefte

Zusätzliche Tests

ISBN 3-19-02.2189-8
© 1977 Max Hueber Verlag München
3 2 1   1981 80 79 78 77
Die jeweils letzten Ziffern bezeichnen Zahl und Jahr des Druckes.
Alle Drucke dieser Auflage können nebeneinander benutzt werden.
Gesamtherstellung: Druckerei Manz AG, Dillingen
Printed in Germany

Inhaltsverzeichnis

Aufbau des Lehrwerks

Zielsetzung

Englisch – Aufbaukurs Technik ist ein Lehrwerk für fortgeschrittene Lernende, die schon über einige Vorkenntnisse sowohl im Umgangsenglisch als auch im fachlichen Bereich verfügen.

Der *Aufbaukurs Technik* schließt nahtlos an den Kenntnisstand an, der nach Durcharbeiten des vorhergehenden Bandes *(Englisch – Grundkurs Technik)* erreicht werden kann. Das Lehrwerk richtet sich aber auch an Lernende, die ihre Vorkenntnisse anderweitig erworben haben.

Die 30 Lektionen des vorliegenden Lehrbuchs sind so abgestuft, daß sie von verhältnismäßig einfachen Strukturen in den ersten Lektionen bis hin zu einer relativ gründlichen Beherrschung der Sprache führen. Das Ziel ist nicht eine eng begrenzte Fachterminologie, sondern eine breit ausgelegte Ausbildung im Gesamtbereich der Sprache, d. h. der Kursteilnehmer soll nach Abschluß des Lehrgangs nicht nur eine bestimmte Anzahl von Fachvokabeln beherrschen, sondern auch in der Lage sein, sich in der Kommunikation sprachlich zu behaupten.

Benutzerkreis

Der *Aufbaukurs Technik* wendet sich in erster Linie an Lernende im beruflichen Schulwesen, an Techniker- und Ingenieurschulen, Fachhochschulen, Technischen Hochschulen sowie an Kursteilnehmer in Volkshochschulen und ähnlichen Bildungseinrichtungen.

Besonders geeignet ist der *Aufbaukurs Technik* auch für die innerbetriebliche Ausbildung in Großbetrieben und anderen Institutionen, da das Arbeitsmaterial ganz auf die Erfordernisse der Praxis zugeschnitten ist.

Textmaterial und Wortschatz

Die Texte sind zum größten Teil Sachtexte, unterbrochen von einigen Dialogen. Es wurde besonderer Wert darauf gelegt, auch die Sachtexte (die ja von Natur aus meist etwas trockener sind) so zu präsentieren, daß das Interesse am Text immer gewahrt bleibt.

Moderne Themen stehen im Vordergrund und sollen neben der Vermittlung des entsprechenden Fachvokabulars und der sprachlichen Strukturen auch

4

gleichzeitig technische Zusammenhänge und – in vielen Fällen – technische Neuerungen vorstellen.

Alle wesentlichen technischen Fachgebiete wurden bei der Auswahl der Texte berücksichtigt, wie z. B. Maschinenbau, Elektrotechnik und Elektronik, Kraftfahrzeugwesen, Eisen und Stahl, Werkzeugbau, Bauwesen, Werkstoffkunde und Weltraumtechnik.

Es versteht sich von selbst, daß in einem Lehrbuch dieses Umfangs nur Ausschnitte aus der Vielzahl der Fachgebiete geboten werden können.

Grammatikteil

Es gibt sicher viele Wege der Grammatikvermittlung, und man muß sich hüten, eine bestimmte Methode als die alleinig effiziente darzustellen*. Im *Aufbaukurs Technik* steht das Beispiel im Mittelpunkt, dem dann, wo nötig und möglich, Darstellungen der Gesetzmäßigkeiten folgen.

Im allgemeinen wird davon ausgegangen, daß der Lernende sich solche Gesetzmäßigkeiten auch über mehrfach wiederholte Beispiele merken kann und nicht in jedem Fall auf kognitive Hilfen angewiesen ist.

Sollte der Kursleiter den Einsatz von Grammatiken bevorzugen, so sei auf die Vorschläge unter „Zusätzliches Material zum Lehrwerk – Grammatiken" verwiesen.

Konzeption der Übungen

Während im *Grundkurs Technik* noch Drillübungen im Vordergrund standen, weichen diese im *Aufbaukurs Technik* immer mehr kommunikations-orientierten Übungen.

Dabei ist zu beachten, daß in diesem Lehrerhandbuch zu jeder Lektion Text- und Transferfragen vorhanden sind, die eine Kommunikation einleiten und unterstützen sollen.

Hinzu kommen Übungen, die den Teilnehmer anregen sollen, einen Mitlernenden zu fragen und mit ihm einen (wenn auch anfangs einfachen) Dialog zu führen.

Der Großteil der Vokabel- und Einsetzübungen befindet sich im Arbeitsbuch.

---

* Diese und verwandte Fragen werden in pragmatischer und praxisnaher Form in dem folgenden Artikel behandelt: Clifford H. Prator: "In Search of a Method" *English Teaching Forum*, January 1976.

Zwischen- und Abschlußtests

Die Tests A, B und C sollen es dem Kursleiter und dem Lernenden ermöglichen, sich ein Bild vom jeweiligen Leistungsstand zu machen. Sie sind als informelle Tests geplant und lassen sich ohne größeren Aufwand im Rahmen des Unterrichts durchführen.

Amerikanisches Englisch

Sicher ist es so, daß die Mehrzahl der Lernenden im Unterricht mit britischem Englisch konfrontiert wird, allein schon aufgrund der Tatsache, daß die meisten Kursleiter britisches Englisch sprechen. Nun wird der Lernende aber in der Praxis – besonders im Bereich des technischen Englisch – unweigerlich auf Kommunikationspartner stoßen, die amerikanisches Englisch sprechen. So muß man es also durchaus als die Aufgabe fortgeschrittener Lehrwerke ansehen, Lernende auf irgendeine Weise darauf vorzubereiten.

Ein solcher Versuch wird immer unvollkommen bleiben, da nur Ausschnitte aus dem weiten Bereich „amerikanisches Englisch" dargestellt werden können und vieles vereinfacht werden muß.

Im *Aufbaukurs Technik* wird folgender Weg beschritten: Die Lektionen 4, 9, 14, 17, 18, 23, 28 und 29, die alle einen amerikanischen Hintergrund haben, werden auf den Tonmaterialien von amerikanischen Sprechern dargeboten. Darüber hinaus findet man in diesem Handbuch bei den entsprechenden Lektionen kurze Hinweise zu den wichtigsten Abweichungen gegenüber dem britischen Englisch und bei Lektion 4 eine ausführlichere (aber immer noch beschränkte) Einführung in die Besonderheiten des amerikanischen Englisch*.

Es empfiehlt sich, die auditiven Hilfsmittel im Unterricht einzusetzen und die Lernenden allmählich mit den Besonderheiten vertraut zu machen.

---

* Ausführlichere Darstellungen findet man an folgenden Stellen: *American English;* Abson Books, Abson, Wick, Bristol, 1975 (nur Wortschatz).
E. Egersten: *Understanding American English;* Klett, Stuttgart, 1974 (Texte mit Cassettenaufnahmen, Erläuterungen).
G. Dahlmann-Resing: „Die Besonderheiten der Aussprache des amerikanischen Englisch und ihre Vermittlung in Lehrwerken"; in: *Zielsprache Englisch,* 1—1978.
H. Galinsky: *Amerikanisches und britisches Englisch;* Reihe: Hueber Hochschulreihe 34; Hueber, München, 1975.
N. Moss: *What's the Difference?* Hutchinson, London, 1973 (Wortschatz mit zahlreichen Anmerkungen).
B. Rink: *Amerikanisch compact;* Hueber, München, 1976 (Wortschatz und Strukturen).

Arbeitshilfen für den Kursleiter

In den meisten Fällen wird es ein Pädagoge sein, der den Unterricht im technischen Englisch übernimmt, seltener ein Ingenieur, der die nötigen Sprachkenntnisse mitbringt.

Man kann durchaus sagen, daß eine technische Ausbildung nicht unbedingt erforderlich ist, wenn man effizienten Unterricht im technischen Englisch erteilen will. Oft ist es gerade umgekehrt: Pädagogisches Geschick wird viel öfter verlangt, da der Unterricht in allererster Linie *Sprach*- und nicht *Sach*unterricht ist.

Der Pädagoge braucht sich also keineswegs unsicher zu fühlen, wenn er kein Ingenieur oder Techniker ist.

Was man aber verlangen muß, ist ein echtes Interesse und Verständnis für technische Vorgänge und den Willen, sich etwas einzuarbeiten. Das bedeutet, daß man sich mit einigen Büchern und eventuell auch einigen Zeitschriften auseinandersetzen muß.

Die folgenden Veröffentlichungen sind eine subjektive Auswahl, von der der Verfasser glaubt, daß sie diese Aufgabe übernehmen kann.

Brockhaus der Naturwissenschaften und der Technik (F. A. Brockhaus, Wiesbaden); Nachschlagewerk, reich illustriert, relativ leicht verständliche Erläuterungen.

Chambers Dictionary of Science and Technology (Chambers, Edinburgh); zwei Taschenbücher mit Begriffserläuterungen aus fast allen Bereichen der Wissenschaft und Technik.

Choice of Careers (Her Majesty's Stationery Office, 49 High Holborn, London WC1V 6HB); Serie von Broschüren, in denen Berufe vorgestellt werden, z. B. Building Crafts, Electrician, Foundry Industry, Iron and Steel, Motor Mechanic, Radio and Television Servicing.

Das Englische Fachwort (von Henry G. Freeman; Girardet, Essen); leicht verständliche Erläuterungen wichtiger Begriffs- und Definitionskomplexe, wie z. B. *pipe/tube, screw/bolt* etc.

Kleine Enzyklopädie Technik (VEB Bibliographisches Institut, Leipzig); preiswertes populärwissenschaftliches Werk mit Einführungen in alle wesentlichen Bereiche der Technik, mit vielen Tabellen, Übersichten und Illustrationen.

Questions and Answers (Newnes-Butterworth, London); Serie von Büchern, die sich mit Automobile Electrical Systems, Automobile Engines, Colour Television, Computers, Diesel Engines, Electronics und vielen anderen Fachgebieten befassen; gute Einführungen in Spezialgebiete, etwas anspruchsvoller, was technische Voraussetzungen angeht.

Folgende Fachzeitschriften lassen sich empfehlen:

Engineering (The Design Council, 28 Haymarket, London SW1Y 4SU); Themen aus vielen Fachgebieten, im allgemeinen nicht zu schwer verständlich.

Popular Mechanics (Box 646, New York, N.Y. 10019); leicht verständliche Artikel aus verschiedenen Bereichen, z. B. Automobiles/Driving, Home and Yard, Electronics/TV/Radio etc.

Popular Motoring (8 Breams Buildings, Fetter Lane, London EC4); Artikel aus dem Automobilbereich in allgemeinverständlicher Aufmachung.

Weitere Informationsmaterialien erhält man in den meisten Fällen von den einschlägigen Firmen, die gewöhnlich gerne bereit sind, Broschüren und Prospekte für Unterrichts- und Studienzwecke zur Verfügung zu stellen.

Aber auch nach einer Einarbeitung erwartet niemand von einem Pädagogen, daß er alle technischen Vorgänge beherrscht. Aus dieser vermeintlichen „Not" kann man jedoch leicht eine Tugend machen: Man bittet einen Kursteilnehmer, der das entsprechende Fachgebiet beherrscht oder auf diesem Gebiet zumindest gut informiert ist, Erläuterungen an der Tafel vorzunehmen (natürlich in Englisch und möglichst mit einer kleinen Skizze). Erfahrungsgemäß sind die Kursteilnehmer gerne bereit, in dieser Weise mitzumachen. Man gewinnt so zusätzliche Übungs- und Kommunikationsmöglichkeiten und bezieht die Kursteilnehmer enger in den Unterricht ein, was sich sehr positiv auf die Motivation auswirken wird.

Hinweise für den Kursteilnehmer

Eine Sprache lernen erfordert aktive Mitarbeit. Mit der meist zu kurzen Unterrichtszeit ist es im allgemeinen nicht getan.

Was kann man als Lernender zusätzlich tun? Da wäre zunächst das Arbeitsbuch, das man in aller Ruhe zu Hause durcharbeiten kann. Die Lösungen zu den Übungen findet man im Anhang, so daß eine sofortige Kontrolle gegeben ist.

Weiterhin empfiehlt es sich, die Texte so oft wie möglich abzuhören (Cassetten, Schallplatten), da sich so der Klang der Sprache gut einprägen kann.

Außerdem sollte man jede andere Gelegenheit wahrnehmen, Englisch zu hören, z. B. Radio- oder Fernsehsendungen, wie die Schulfunksendungen für Fortgeschrittene. Sprachlich anspruchsvoller sind die Sendungen des BFBS (= British Forces Broadcasting Service) und des AFN (= American Forces Network). Man sollte sich durch anfängliche Schwierigkeiten nicht entmutigen lassen, denn in der Praxis hat es sich gezeigt, daß im Laufe der Zeit doch mit Erfolgen (d. h. mit größerem Verständnis der gesprochenen Sprache) zu rechnen ist.

Auch das Lesen einer Zeitung gehört zu den nützlichen Übungsmöglichkeiten für Fortgeschrittene, auch wenn es sich um nicht-technische Beiträge handelt.

Auch die populärwissenschaftlichen Zeitschriften (siehe auch unter „Arbeitshilfen für den Kursleiter") eignen sich ganz vorzüglich als Lesematerial für Fortgeschrittene.

Immer muß man sich vor Augen halten, daß Sprachenlernen Ausdauer erfordert: Erfolge wechseln oft mit Zeiten ab, in denen man glaubt, nicht mehr weiter zu kommen. Dann heißt es, diese Zeiten zu überwinden und auf das nächste (sicher kommende) „Hoch" zu warten.

Einsatz des Lehrwerks im Unterricht

Kommunikationsübungen

Lehrgänge und Kurse für Fortgeschrittene müssen vor allem ein Ziel ansteuern: die Kommunikationsfähigkeit, d. h. die Fähigkeit, Englisch verstehen, sprechen und schreiben zu können. Das gilt auch für technisches Englisch, da die Situationen, in denen ein Ingenieur oder Techniker Kommunikationsfähigkeit braucht, bei weitem überwiegen. Außerdem bringt das Verstehen und Sprechen der fremden Sprache Erfolgserlebnisse, die reines Vokabelwissen und Grammatikkenntnisse nicht vermitteln können.

Es ist daher wichtig, bei jedem neuen Text die schon vorher erwähnten Text- und Transferfragen einzusetzen (siehe die Ausführungen zu den einzelnen Lektionen in diesem Handbuch).

Weiterhin ist der richtige Einsatz der Kommunikationsübungen wichtig, wie z. B. Übung 6, Lektion 2. Hier kommt es darauf an, die Lernenden dahin zu führen, nach und nach das in den ersten Lektionen noch etwas starre Schema zu verlassen und von sich aus weiterzufragen. Das kann man nur erreichen, wenn man es als Kursleiter mehrfach durchgespielt hat, etwa nach folgendem Muster:

Kursleiter zu Teilnehmer 1: What do you think about hi-fi fans? — *(Antwort des Teilnehmers)* — I see. Well, would you say you're a hi-fi fan? — *(Antwort des Teilnehmers)* — No? Well, do you like listening to music? — *(Antwort des Teilnehmers)* — Now ask Mr So-and-so what he thinks about hi-fi-fans ...

Teilnehmer 2: Well, I think ... *(etc.)*

Kursleiter zu Teilnehmer 1: Now ask him whether he is a hi-fi fan ...

Beim nächsten Durchgang mit ähnlichen Fragestellungen wird dann schon ein Nachhaken seitens des Kursleiters weniger nötig sein, und bald wird die Übung fast automatisch ablaufen.

Gerade bei den ersten Lektionen darf man keine Scheu haben, Übungen zu wiederholen. Es wäre z. B. denkbar, vor Beginn der neuen Stunde (mit einer neuen Lektion) die alte Lektion kurz zu wiederholen, indem man die Text- und Transferfragen (in etwas abgewandelter Form) und eine Kommunikationsübung noch einmal durchgeht.

Einsatz audiovisueller Mittel

Die den Lektionen zugeordneten Illustrationen dienen nicht nur der Auflockerung, sondern haben in den meisten Fällen eine methodische Funktion. Sie sollten daher auch, wenn möglich, in den Unterrichtsablauf einbezogen werden. Das geschieht am besten, indem man Fragen zu den Illustrationen stellt und sie von den Teilnehmern beantworten läßt.

Nimmt man z. B. die Illustration zu "What's new on the market (1)?" in der ersten Lektion, so lassen sich folgende Fragen stellen:

What is the man doing?
Where is he standing?
Why are the pipes being insulated?
What are they being insulated with?
Why is such a snap-on system more efficient?

Dies kann in Verbindung mit den sowieso fälligen Text- und Transferfragen oder aber auch als getrennter Durchgang erfolgen.

In fortgeschritteneren Kursen (etwa von der zweiten Hälfte des Buches an) wäre auch der Einsatz von zusätzlichen Transparentmodellen und Arbeitstransparenten denkbar. Solche Hilfsmittel werden auf den Overheadprojektor gelegt und lassen Bewegungsabläufe sichtbar werden.

Die Firma idf-Unterrichtstechnologie (Postfach 5469, 7800 Freiburg) stellt durchsichtige Funktionsmodelle her, und zwar zu den vielfältigsten technischen

Vorgängen aus den Bereichen Kraftfahrzeugtechnik, Mechanik, Technologie. Wenn man z. B. das Modell eines Viertaktmotors auf den Overheadprojektor legt, so kann man durch das Bewegen der entsprechenden Teile sehr anschaulich die Funktionsabläufe erklären bzw. von einem Kursteilnehmer erklären lassen (mit den entsprechenden Vokabelvorgaben).

Zum Einsatz der Arbeitstransparente der Firma Tobifo (Rosenweg 12, 6901 Neckarsteinach) braucht man einen Polarisationsfilter, der mitgeliefert wird. Auch hier gibt es eine Reihe von brauchbaren Transparenten aus dem technisch-naturwissenschaftlichen Bereich.

Zu beiden Systemen muß allerdings gesagt werden, daß sie wegen ihres Preises (ca. 20,– bis 80,– DM pro Modell) wohl nur von der Schule, Firma oder Institution und nicht vom Kursleiter selbst beschafft werden können.

Der Einsatz der Tonmaterialien im Unterricht ist dringend zu empfehlen, damit der Teilnehmer nicht nur die Stimme des Kursleiters hört. Außerdem wird er auf diese Weise ja auch die amerikanischen Versionen kennenlernen, die ihm sonst entgehen würden. Um aus dem Abspielen eines Textes eine echte Hörverständnisübung zu machen, empfiehlt es sich, einen neuen Text ohne vorherige Erläuterungen vorzuspielen und dann die Text- und Transferfragen zu stellen. Danach kann man dann die Erläuterungen folgen lassen. Dieses Verfahren eignet sich aber nicht so sehr für die ersten zwei oder drei Lektionen, da der Kursteilnehmer etwas Zeit braucht, um sich an den Arbeitsrhythmus zu gewöhnen*.

Einsprachigkeit

Über diese methodische Streitfrage ist schon viel geschrieben worden, so daß hier keine weiteren Argumente vorgebracht werden sollen. Es soll nur versucht werden, eine unterrichtsgerechte und praxisnahe Kompromißlösung zu finden. Sicher *muß* der Unterricht auf dieser fortgeschrittenen Stufe weitestgehend einsprachig, d. h. Englisch, ablaufen. Das heißt aber nicht, daß der *gelegentliche* Einsatz der Muttersprache verwerflich wäre. Es gibt nämlich Unterrichtssituationen, in denen der Einsatz der Muttersprache sinnvoll erscheint, z. B. bei der Textpräsentation, wenn neue Vokabeln zu erläutern sind. Aus Gründen der Unterrichtsökonomie empfiehlt es sich, bestimmte Wörter zu übersetzen und auf eine englische Begriffsbestimmung zu verzichten, da sie zu viel Zeit erfor-

---

* Ausführlichere Erläuterungen zu diesem Punkt und zu allen anderen Didaktik- und Methodikproblemen findet man in folgendem Buch: Burgschmidt/Götz/Hoffmann/ Hohmann/Schrand: *Englisch als Zielsprache;* Hueber, München, 1975.

dert und das Verstehen des Begriffs doch nicht immer sichergestellt ist. Gerade im technischen Bereich gibt es viele Fälle, wo dies zu empfehlen ist.

Aus diesem Grunde (und um dem Lernenden die häusliche Arbeit zu erleichtern) sind die Worterläuterungen zweisprachig gehalten. Im vorliegenden Handbuch findet man zu den einzelnen Lektionen einige einsprachige Wortdefinitionen, die man nach eigenem Gutdünken in den Unterricht einfließen lassen kann.

Zusätzliches Material zum Lehrwerk

Arbeitsbuch

Um das Lehrbuch von Übungen zu entlasten, die man recht gut auch zu Hause machen kann, wurden die meisten Vokabel-, Präpositions- und Einsetzübungen ins Arbeitsbuch zum *Aufbaukurs Technik* verlegt. Hinzu kommen weiterführende Texte, die in den meisten Fällen an die Themen der Lehrbuchlektionen anknüpfen. Das Arbeitsbuch enthält einen Schlüssel zu den Übungen und läßt somit eine sofortige Kontrolle zu.

Compact-Cassetten, Schallplatten und Tonbänder

Die Tonmaterialien enthalten die Aufnahmen aller Lesetexte und dienen in erster Linie der Schulung des Hörverständnisses. Sie sind sowohl für den Einsatz im Unterricht als auch für die häusliche Arbeit gedacht. Die Lektionen 4, 9, 14, 17, 18, 23, 28 und 29 werden von amerikanischen Sprechern gesprochen.

Lernwörterbuch

Das Lernwörterbuch zum *Aufbaukurs Technik* enthält alle Vokabeln des Lehrbuchs und des Arbeitsbuchs sowie die Erläuterungen und Aussprachehilfen zu den Maßeinheiten und Tabellen im Anhang des Lehrbuchs. Die Eintragungen (Englisch-Deutsch) sind so gehalten, daß der Lernende die Vokabeln möglichst im Zusammenhang mit einem Begriff oder einem erläuternden Satz vorfindet.

Grammatiken

Sollten weitergehende kognitive Hilfen erforderlich sein, so sind folgende Bücher empfehlenswert: H. G. Hoffmann: *Englische Taschengrammatik* (Hueber), besonders für Lernende; H. G. Hoffmann: *Englische Mindestgrammatik* (Hueber), für fortgeschrittene Lernende und Kursleiter (als Arbeitshilfe).

Auswahl zweisprachiger technischer Wörterbücher

Technik allgemein

De Vries/Herrmann: *Technical and Engineering Dictionary*, Deutsch-Englisch/ Englisch-Deutsch (Brandstetter, Wiesbaden).

Ernst: *Wörterbuch der Industriellen Technik*, Deutsch-Englisch / Englisch-Deutsch (Brandstetter, Wiesbaden).

Freeman: *Technisches Taschenwörterbuch*, Deutsch-Englisch/Englisch-Deutsch (Hueber, München).

Automobilbau

Freeman: *Taschenwörterbuch Kraftfahrzeugtechnik*, Deutsch-Englisch (Hueber, München).

Tutzauer: *Automobiltechnisches Wörterbuch*, Englisch-Französisch-Deutsch/ Deutsch-Englisch-Französisch/Französisch-Englisch-Deutsch (Heymanns, Köln).

Wyhlidal: *Kraftfahrzeugtechnisches Wörterbuch*, Englisch-Deutsch/Deutsch-Englisch (International Language Service Est., FL-9490 Vaduz, Postfach 225).

Elektrotechnik/Elektronik

Herrmann: *Electricity/Electronics – Minimum Wordage*, Englisch-Deutsch (Hueber, München).

Höhn: *Wörterbuch der Elektroindustrie*, Deutsch-Englisch/Englisch-Deutsch (Econ, Düsseldorf).

Schwenkhagen/Meinhold: *Wörterbuch Elektrotechnik und Elektronik,* Deutsch-Englisch/Englisch-Deutsch (Girardet, Essen).

Wernicke: *Wörterbuch der Elektronik, Nachrichten- und Elektrotechnik* (Wernicke, München).

Ingenieurbau/Baumaschinen

Bucksch: *Wörterbuch für Ingenieurbau und Baumaschinen,* Deutsch-Englisch/Englisch-Deutsch (Bauverlag, Wiesbaden/Berlin).

Maschinenbau/Eisen und Stahl

Freeman: *Fachwörterbuch Spanende Werkzeugmaschinen,* Deutsch-Englisch; *Dictionary of Metal-Cutting Tools,* Englisch-Deutsch (Girardet, Essen).

Freeman: *Spezialwörterbuch Maschinenwesen,* Deutsch-Englisch / Englisch-Deutsch (Girardet, Essen).

Freeman: *Taschenwörterbuch Eisen und Stahl,* Deutsch-Englisch / Englisch-Deutsch (Hueber, München).

Zusätzliche Informationen
Text- und Transferfragen
Methodische Hinweise und Schlüssel

LESSON 1

Zusätzliche Informationen

brain-storming: "a conference technique of solving specific problems, developing new ideas, etc., by unrestrained participation in discussion".

insulation (*Verb:* insulate ['insjuleit]): Isolierung, Isolation im technischen Sinne; sonst: isolation [aisəu'leiʃən], isolate ['aisəleit].

fiber glass (*Br.:* fibre glass): streng genommen eine Handelsmarke; genereller Begriff: glass fibre; Definition: "Glass melted and then drawn out by steam through special bushings into fibres of 5–10 micrometres diameter, which may be spun continuously into threads and woven into tapes and cloths by normal process, or may be formed into pads and quiltings, rigid, bitumen-bonded or loose".

Weitere Fragen aus dem Originaltext: Can we buy a similar product at cheaper cost elsewhere? / Could we have another of our products made at the same time as this one – thus saving cost? / Is there more on the product than we actually require? / Must the product have the same element of strength and durability *all the way through*? / When did we last visit the supplier to find out if he is giving us the best of his facilities?

Text- und Transferfragen	**Some questions for a brain-storming session:** Can you explain what a brain-storming session is? Why was the list of idea-stimulators drawn up? Have you ever attended such a session? (When? What was the problem? Who was there?) Do you think brain-storming sessions are a good idea? When do you think a company should have a brain-storming session? (When there is a problem? When they need new ideas? Regularly every week?) **What's new on the market?** What has been developed by the American company? What can the new system be used for?

15

Is it difficult to install?
What other advantages can you think of?
What about high temperatures?

Methodische Hinweise und Schlüssel

1 a. If you go to England, you'll have to get used to driving on the left.
b. If you want to work for this company, you'll have to get used to working
overtime. **c.** If you want to be competitive, you'll have to get used to scrap
materials. **d.** If you want to stay in business, you'll have to get used to buying
bulk. **e.** If you want to work in a team, you'll have to get used to discussions.

2 a. developed **b.** attended **c.** designed **d.** used **e.** helped **f.** supplied

3 a. No, I'm sure he didn't. **b.** No, I'm sure she isn't. **c.** No, I'm sure they
won't. **d.** No, I'm sure it isn't. **e.** No, I'm sure he can't. **f.** No, I'm sure it
doesn't. **g.** No, I'm sure they couldn't. **h.** No, I'm sure he doesn't. **i.** No, I'm
sure it doesn't.

4 Mit dieser und der folgenden Übung beginnt eine Phase, die den Teilnehmer immer mehr zur freien Konversation, zum freien Sprechen, hinführen soll.
Verstreut über die nächsten Lektionen folgen immer wieder Übungen dieser
Art, bis am Ende auch die hier noch relativ straffe strukturelle Führung weg-
fällt.

Zur praktischen Durchführung: Im Gegensatz zu den Text- und Transferfragen,
die ja vom Kursleiter gestellt werden, sollen die hier beginnenden Kommunikationsübungen zwischen den Teilnehmern ablaufen, d. h. ein Teilnehmer fragt
und ein anderer antwortet.

Natürlich kann man bei größeren Gruppen nicht bei jeder Übung reihum alle
Teilnehmer fragen und antworten lassen. Man sollte aber darauf achten, daß
alle Teilnehmer im Laufe einer Unterrichtseinheit wenigstens einmal freiere
Fragen gestellt haben.

b. Are you sure it's the right shape? **c.** Could you reduce the unit cost by
buying bulk? **d.** Have you made it as safe as possible? **e.** Are you sure it's
sufficiently heat resistant? **f.** Do you think a lighter material would prevent
corrosion?

5 Siehe auch methodische Hinweise unter 4. Hier und bei den meisten folgenden Übungen dieser Art werden die angegebenen Lösungen nur Vorschläge
sein können, die beliebigen Variationen unterliegen.

16

b. Must it be weatherproof? **c.** Could it be made of scrap materials? **d.** Could we reduce the unit cost by buying bulk? **e.** Is it sufficiently heat resistant? **f.** Could we design it better? **g.** Is it as safe as it should be? **h.** Are we sure it is exactly the right shape? **i.** Would a lighter material prevent corrosion? **j.** Does it open and shut easily?

6 Sollten Gruppenzusammensetzung und Zeit der Teilnehmer es zulassen, kann man Übersetzungsübungen auch gut als Hausaufgaben einsetzen.

a. I've attended (*oder:* taken part in) many brain-storming sessions in my life. **b.** We must (*oder:* have to) get used to making (*oder:* producing; *oder:* manufacturing) our machines of lighter materials. **c.** Couldn't we have reduced the unit cost? **d.** If we had talked about (*oder:* discussed) these problems earlier, we wouldn't have (any) difficulties now.

LESSON 2

Zusätzliche Informationen

frequency response: "the width of the sound spectrum (in Hz) that the speaker will reproduce; 60–15,000 Hz is quite sufficient".

hertz (Hz): "unit of frequency, equal to one cycle per second".

cross-over frequency: "in loudspeaker systems and multi-amplifier audio installations, the borderline frequencies between low/medium range and medium/high range speakers or amplifiers".

cross-over network: "auxiliary parts in a speaker system include the cross-over network and, sometimes, one or more level controls; the cross-over network is an electronic circuit which splits up the sound spectrum into the required number of ways — low and mid/high range in a 2-way system, low, mid and high in a 3-way".

Quellen für zusätzliches Arbeitsmaterial: Die großen Hi-Fi- und Elektronik-firmen geben umfangreiche und oft gut im Unterricht einsetzbare Informations-broschüren und -prospekte heraus, z. B. Sony (9 West 57th Street, New York, N.Y. 10019); Altec (1515 S. Manchester Ave., Anaheim, CA 92803); Bose Corporation (The Mountain, Framingham, MA 01701); Pioneer Electronic Corporation (Shriro House, The Ridgeway, Iver/Buckinghamshire SLO 9JL).

Text- und Transferfragen

Why did one of the two persons in the text build a loud-speaker system?

Was it a very powerful system?

What was included in the kit?

Did the other person in the text buy a loudspeaker system?

What is a woofer? What is a tweeter?

Why is a very high frequency response more or less useless?

What do you need to build an enclosure?

Do you think you could build a loudspeaker system?

Is a loudspeaker kit always cheaper than a loudspeaker you buy?

Methodische Hinweise und Schlüssel

1 A1+B1 / A2+B2 / A3+B5 / A4+B3 / A5+B4

2 a. You should have repaired the engine. **b.** You should have done a bit of reading. **c.** You should have gone to Coventry. **d.** You should have used a different material. **e.** You should have attended a brain-storming session or two. **f.** You should have designed a better engine. **g.** You should have known the new SI units. **h.** You should have worked overtime. **i.** You should have made the machine more easily portable.

3 a. system **b.** power **c.** materials **d.** network **e.** circuits **f.** shape

4 a. And what about the enclosure? Did you build it yourself, too? – Yes, certainly. I built it last Friday. **b.** And what about the amplifiers? Did you assemble them yourself, too? – Yes, certainly. I assembled them in my holiday. **c.** And what about the body? Did you paint it yourself, too? – Yes, certainly. I painted it over the weekend. **d.** And what about the pipe insulation system? Did you design it yourself, too? – Yes, certainly. I designed it when I worked in Birmingham.

5 a. When we arrived yesterday, the chief engineer wasn't there. **b.** When I met her in London, she wasn't interested in loudspeakers. **c.** Before he came to Germany, he had worked in America for a few (*oder:* some) years. **d.** Yesterday I spent five hours repairing the tape recorder and the amplifier. **e.** Were you in the workshop yesterday evening? **f.** Did you work overtime last week? **g.** Yesterday I attended several "brain-storming sessions". **h.** Did you speak with the chief engineer yesterday? **i.** Can the insulation material (which) you showed me last week also be used for high temperatures? (*oder:* ... be used for high temperatures, too?) **j.** Why didn't the mechanic repair the car when you were in the workshop? **k.** When did he build in the cross-over network? **l.** When did he give you the kit? **m.** Why didn't you call me yesterday? **n.** Are you really interested in an amplifier? – Yes, certainly.

6 Diese Übung kann man mehrmals durchlaufen lassen (am besten aber nicht mehrmals hintereinander), um möglichst vielen Teilnehmern Gelegenheit zum Sprechen zu geben.

a. Were you in the workshop last Sunday? **b.** Can you build a loudspeaker system? **c.** Do you know what a cross-over network is? **d.** Were you in England last year? **e.** Can you repair a tape deck? **f.** What do you think about (*oder:* of) hi-fi fans?

LESSON 3

Zusätzliche Informationen

Offshore drilling

Condeep construction technique: "The platform foundation raft is usually built in a dry dock, although some of the smaller designs may be constructed on floating barges. The remainder of the concrete structure is completed in floating condition at a deep water site. Steel skirts which are designed to penetrate the sea bed are erected on a solid foundation in the dock. The dome shaped cell bottoms and the lower part of the cell walls are then cast. By means of advanced methods using prefabricated concrete elements as shuttering, building time is reduced without affecting strength and tightness requirements for the structure. While construction of the foundation raft is in progress in the dry dock a deep water site is prepared in the fjord. The necessary moorings include heavy chain cables secured to mud anchors and to a winch ashore. As soon as the foundation raft is completed the dry dock is filled with water, the sheet pile wall is removed and the raft is towed to the deep water site and moored.

At the deep water site pouring of the cell walls of the substructure continues to full height using slip forms (= *Gleitschalungen*). Ballast water is added during the pouring operation in order to keep a convenient freeboard. The next operation is to erect forms, reinforce and pour the top domes.

The final and probably the most exacting concrete work is the construction of the approx. 100 m high towers which are to support the deck. The towers, which are slipformed simultaneously, have varying diameter and wall thickness. The exact positioning of the towers is ensured by the use of laser beams.

Upon termination of the concrete works the towers are capped with special steel connectors and equipment for ballast handling and oil storage is installed.

While building of the concrete structure is in progress the deck is constructed at a suitable shipyard or construction site.

After completion, including the installation of all the drilling and production equipment, the deck is towed on pontoons to the deck mounting site in a deep sheltered fjord.

Upon arrival of the deck structure, the final preparations are made for the installation of the deck. The concrete structure is submerged, leaving approx. 5 m of the concrete towers above water line. The deck is then floated over the concrete structure and kept in correct position by tug boats. The concrete structure is thereafter deballasted, lifting the deck structure off the barges to a predetermined height.

The CONDEEP ist now ready for towage to the offshore field.

Five or six ocean going tugs totalling 60 000—80 000 hp are required. In calm weather the towing speed is approx. 2 knots. On arrival at the field the tugs are arranged in a starshaped formation. The platform is then towed to the exact location and submerged by ballasting of the cells.

When the skirts have penetrated the sea bed the structure is levelled by varying the water levels in the cells and possibly by varying the water pressure in the skirts compartments. It has proved possible to obtain an inclination of less than o.1 degree.

Finally, the foundation area is grouted and the drilling of wells can start."

(A. S. Høyer-Ellefsen, Oslo)

A simple experiment

Erläuterungen zum Experiment: "The gas obtained by heating coal in this way is called coal gas. Until recently the gas used in cooking stoves, and in some places for lighting, was coal gas, but now it is often mixed with natural gas, or with fuel gases which are the byproducts of some industrial processes such as the petroleum industry. In some places natural gas only is used. So now we call the gas supplied to our houses (or to the laboratory) not coal gas, but 'town gas'. You will have found a tarry liquid collected in the tube B. This is coal-tar, and from it a large number of useful products can be obtained by distillation. Some of these are benzene, toluene, and naphthalene, and from them many more very important chemicals can be manufactured.

The solid product left behind in the tube after the coal has been heated is coke. In these days coal is very often heated like this just to get the coke and the coal-tar, the gas being merely a by-product. Coke is a very useful smokeless fuel and is used a great deal in the smelting of metals as a reducing agent. It is nearly pure carbon."

Text- und Transferfragen

Where will much of the oil and gas we need come from?

How much (in per cent) will come from under the ocean bed?

What sort of equipment is needed to get the oil out of the ground?

Can you give some examples of places where offshore drilling takes place?

What do you remember about the construction of the Condeep platform? *(Je nach Notwendigkeit können weitere Hilfestellungen folgen: What about the construction material? What about storage capacity? etc. etc.*

Methodische Hinweise und Schlüssel

1 a. wrong b. right c. wrong d. wrong e. right f. wrong

2 a. about b. from c. of d. out to e. of ... over f. of ... from under

3 a. is b. be c. are d. is e. be f. be g. be h. is

4 a. Have they painted the walls? – No, they haven't, but they're going to paint them on Wednesday. b. Have they installed the computer? – No, they haven't, but they're going to install it when they come back from Birmingham. c. Have they built the loudspeaker system? – No, they haven't, but they're going to build it next weekend. d. Have they checked the integrated circuits? – No, they haven't, but they're going to check them on Monday morning.

5 a. The electric motor is checked in the workshop. b. The components are produced in the factory. c. The brain-storming session is held in the office. d. The bodies are painted in the garage.

6 a. side b. side c. sites d. site e. sides f. site

LESSON 4

Zusätzliche Informationen

American English

In dieser Lektion soll zum erstenmal etwas stärker auf das amerikanische Englisch eingegangen werden. Auf den Tonmaterialien werden daher amerikanische Sprecher zu hören sein.
Hinzu kommen die folgenden Erläuterungen, die natürlich sehr knapp gehalten werden müssen, um den gesetzten Rahmen nicht zu sprengen (es sei noch einmal auf die Literaturhinweise auf Seite 6 hingewiesen):

■ Schreibweise

Wenn zwei Varianten hintereinander angegeben werden, so ist die erste im betreffenden Sprachbereich häufiger.

1 Konsonantenverdoppelung

American English	British English
kidnaped / kidnapped	kidnapped
kidnaper / kidnapper	kidnapper
worshiped / worshipped	worshipped
canceled / cancelled	cancelled
dialed / dialled	dialled
leveling / levelling	levelling
traveled / travelled	travelled

(Anmerkung: Verben, die auf der letzten Silbe betont werden – z. B. control, annul – haben auch im amerikanischen Englisch ein Doppel-l: controlled, annulled.)

2 Bindestrich: Im amerikanischen Englisch werden zusammengesetzte Wörter (besonders, wenn das erste Element auf *-ing* endet) gewöhnlich ohne Bindestrich geschrieben: milling machine, landing field. Ein ähnlicher Trend ist allerdings auch im britischen Englisch zu beobachten.

3 Endung -or oder -our

American English	British English
behavior / behaviour	behaviour
color / colour	colour
favor / favour	favour
harbor / harbour	harbour
humor / humour	humour
vapor / vapour	vapour

4 Endung -se oder -ce

American English	British English
defense / defence	defence
license / licence (n)	licence (n)
license / licence (vb)	license (vb)
practice / practise (vb)	practise (vb)

5 Endung -er oder -re

American English	British English
center / centre	centre
fiber glass / fibre glass	fibre glass
liter / litre	litre
meter / metre	metre

6 Sonderformen

American English	British English
carburetor	carburettor / carburetter / carburetor
catalog / catalogue	catalogue
check	cheque
curb	kerb
gram	gramme / gram
program	programme / program
tire	tyre / tire
vise (= Schraubstock)	vice

(Die folgenden Sonderformen sind nicht allgemein anerkannt, werden jedoch häufig verwandt:)

thoro / thorough	thorough
tho / though	though
thru / through	through

■ Wortschatz

American English	British English	
back-up lights	reversing lights	Rückfahrscheinwerfer
electric cord	flex	Litze, Schnur
elevator	lift	Aufzug
fender	wing, mudguard	Kotflügel
flashlight	torch	Taschenlampe
freight car	goods wagon	Güterwagen
gas (= gasoline)	petrol	Benzin

■ Wortschatz

hood	bonnet	Motorhaube
parking lot	car park	Parkplatz
pick-up truck	light lorry	Kleinlaster
trash can	dustbin	Mülleimer
truck	lorry	Lastwagen
trunk	boot	Kofferraum
windshield	windscreen	Windschutzscheibe

■ Aussprache

1 [ɑ:] – [ɔ]

	AMERICAN ENGLISH	BRITISH ENGLISH
hot	[hɑ:t]	[hɔt]
shop	[ʃɑ:p]	[ʃɔp]
spot	[spɑ:t]	[spɔt]
ton	[tɑ:n]	[tɔn]
top	[tɑ:p]	[tɔp]

2 [æ] – [o:]

	AMERICAN ENGLISH	BRITISH ENGLISH
after	['æ:ftər]	['ɑ:ftə]
craft	[kræ:ft]	[krɑ:ft]
half	[hæ:f]	[hɑ:f]

3 [r] – [—]

	AMERICAN ENGLISH	BRITISH ENGLISH
car	[kɑ:r]	[kɑ:]
card	[kɑ:rd]	[kɑ:d]
far	[fɑ:r]	[fɑ:]
for	[fɔ:r]	[fɔ:]

24

4 [ɔ:r] – [ʌr]

	American English	British English
current	['kɔ:rənt]	['kʌrənt]
hurry	['hɔ:ri]	['hʌri]
worry	['wɔ:ri]	['wʌri]

5 [u:] – [ju:]

	American English	British English
new	[nu:]	[nju:]
student	['stu:dənt]	['stju:dənt]

6 Endung -ile

	American English	British English
fragile	['frædzl]	['frædzail]
tensile	['tensl]	['tensail]

7 [d] – [t]

	American English	British English
beautiful	['bju:dəfəl]	['bju:təful]
bottle	[bɑ:dl]	[bɔtl]
partner	['pɑ:rdnə]	['pɑ:tnə]

8 Endungen -ary, -ory, etc.

	American English	British English
dictionary	['dikʃəneri]	['dikʃənri / 'dikʃənəri]
inventory	['invəntɔri]	['invəntri]

	AMERICAN ENGLISH	BRITISH ENGLISH
advertisement	[ædvər'taizmənt / əd'və:tismənt]	[əd'və:tismənt]
anti-	['æntai / 'ænti-]	['ænti-]
been	[bin]	[bi:n]
issue	['iʃu:]	['isju / 'iʃu:]
leisure	['li:ʒər]	['leʒə]
lever	['levər / 'li:vər)	['li:və]
measure	['meʒər / 'meiʒər]	['·meʒə]
multi-	['mʌlti- / 'mʌltai-]	['mʌlti-]
patent	['pætnt]	['peitnt / 'pætnt]
z (= Buchstabe)	[zi:]	[zed]

■ Strukturen

AMERICAN ENGLISH	BRITISH ENGLISH
I saw her around four weeks ago.	I saw her about four weeks ago.
That was a real good drink!	That was a really good drink!
He can work real fast.	He can work really fast.
I don't like him any.	I don't like him at all.
All of these tools are mine.	All these tools are mine.
Do you have any children?	Have you (got) any children?
Do you have enough money?	Have you (got) enough money?
John just bought a new camera.	John has just bought a new camera.
I couldn't help but fall asleep.	I couldn't help falling asleep.
He jumped out the window.	He jumped out of the window.
I recommended that he come here by eight o'clock.	I recommended that he should come here by eight o'clock.

Electronics training at home

Der folgende Zusatztext aus einer Broschüre des Cleveland Institute of Electronics verdeutlicht die Zusammenhänge um die FCC license courses:

Why we have FCC Licenses

The Congress gave to the Federal Communications Commission (FCC) the responsibility to "police" the airwaves in the United States. At the same time, it gave the FCC the authority to make the rules and regulations needed to fulfill that responsibility. This guide is concerned with those rules and regulations as they affect technicians.

The latest FCC report shows over 8,000,000 transmitters operating in the United States, exclusive of the Armed Forces. Imagine the confusion if just anyone were permitted to operate and maintain these transmitters! Frequencies would overlap ... signals would be distorted ... directional stations would be non-directional and valuable equipment might be damaged or destroyed.

So, the FCC must be assured that only qualified technicians maintain and operate transmission equipment. From the lowest amateur category to the chief engineer of a powerful radio or television station, the FCC demands a technical understanding of the fundamentals of electronics.

Through the licensing examination, the FCC is assured that only qualified technicians obtain the respected FCC License. That's why the FCC "ticket" is generally considered by industry as government certification of technical competence.

How you profit from your FCC License

People with an FCC License nearly always have an advantage over the unlicensed. In the communications field, law requires a license in many jobs. Some employers prefer the licensed person because the license indicates a thorough and tested knowledge of electronics. The holder of a first or second class "ticket" has already proven his technical capabilities.

As you read this booklet, you will see *why* the licensed person enjoys these advantages. Just passing the examination is an achievement. Conducted by the FCC, it thoroughly covers theory of electronics and the related math. Since all electronics equipment is based on the same fundamental circuits, a license holder is certified for work in any area of electronics.

U.S. Government certification of your technical competence can bring you many thousands of dollars of additional income during your working career.

the Greek letter μ: [mju:]

resistance: "a property of a conductor by virtue of which the passage of current is opposed, causing electric energy to be transformed into heat"

resistor: "a device, the primary purpose of which is to introduce resistance into an electric circuit"

Some questions from the FCC examination

1 Crystal microphones may be damaged by high temperature and humidity and they do not generally have the frequency response required for commercial broadcasting.

2 e) ohm

3 Wow is a fluctuation of turntable or tape speed. A broadcast turntable requires approximately 1/3 turn before the torque of the motor can bring the turntable up to proper speed. If a record is not properly cued or "backed up" 1/3 turn, the listeners will hear distortion when the record is started. The change in pitch of a record as the turntable speed varies actually sounds like a "wow"*.

4 Power output does not change.

5 North.

Text- und Transferfragen

Why is Herbert interested in correspondence courses?
What is Jack studying at the moment?
What other courses does the correspondence school offer?
What do you think is a programmed course?
Have you ever taken part in a correspondence course?
  (If yes: When? What subjects?)
Do you think it is possible to become a technician by
  studying at a correspondence school? (Why? Why not?)

Methodische Hinweise und Schlüssel

1 Man sollte es als Kursleiter nicht bei der Frage-und-Antwort-Übung bewenden lassen, sondern über das *No, I haven't* oder *Yes, I have* hinaus in eine echte Kommunikation überleiten. Dazu muß man die Kursteilnehmer anleiten, nachzuhaken, z. B.: *Have you ever studied anything at home? – Yes, I have. – What was that? – Well, I studied English at home some years ago...*
a. Have you ever studied anything at home? b. Do you know a good correspondence school in Germany? c. Do you think it is possible to study electronics at home? d. Do you know what a programmed course is? e. Do you know anything about Ohm's Law? f. Do you think it should be possible to study at home to become a technician?

2 a. college b. abbreviation c. technology d. solder e. computer f. technician

3 In unregelmäßigen Abständen folgen schriftliche Übungen dieser oder ähnlicher Art. Sie bieten sich als Hausaufgaben an, wenn dieser zusätzliche Arbeitsaufwand im Rahmen des Möglichen liegt.
Eine „Lösung" kann bei solchen Aufgaben natürlich nicht vorgegeben werden, da die möglichen Reaktionen und Aussagen zu vielfältig sind. Der Kursleiter wird die fertigen Arbeiten individuell nachsehen müssen.

4 a. I may have some oil for you but I certainly haven't got any petrol. b. I may have some leaflets for you but I certainly haven't got any operating

---

* wow [wau] = „wimmern"; wow and flutter = Gleichlaufschwankungen (bei einem Plattenspieler oder Tonbandgerät).

manuals. **c.** I may have some insulation material for you but I certainly haven't got any coal. **d.** I may have some plugs for you but I certainly haven't got any sockets.

5 a. anything (*oder auch:* something) . . . some **b.** anything **c.** some **d.** something **e.** any **f.** some

6 a. do . . . get . . . measuring **b.** studying **c.** Constructing **d.** built **e.** supporting . . . used . . . drilling

7 a. I wonder why he didn't repair the TV set this morning. **b.** I wonder why he didn't study electronics last year. **c.** I wonder why he didn't do any practical work at home. **d.** I wonder why he didn't attend the brain-storming session yesterday. **e.** I wonder why he didn't use the drilling machine when he was in the workshop last Monday. **f.** I wonder why he didn't buy the new loudspeaker last week.

LESSON 5

Zusätzliche Informationen

Das nebenstehende elektromagnetische Spektrum zeigt die relative Position der Mikrowellen, die für den *mirowave oven* verwendet werden:

Frequency Cycles per second	
10^{22}	GAMMA
10^{20}	
10^{18}	X-RAY
10^{16}	ULTRA VIOLETT
10^{14}	VISIBLE LIGHT
10^{12}	INFRARED
10^{10}	MICROWAVE
10^8	
10^6	BROADCAST BAND
10^4	

Text- und	How do microwaves cook?
Transferfragen	Can you give some examples of electro-magnetic energy?
	How do microwaves cook?
	Have you ever seen a microwave oven?
	Why are microwave ovens not dangerous?

What's new on the market?
Who has developed the new system?
Where will it be used?
Can you explain how it works?

Methodische Hinweise und Schlüssel

1 (1) oven (2) interested (3) advantages (4) save (5) do (6) energy (7) waves (8) frequency (9) length (10) mine (11) couple (12) foil (13) quite (14) reflect (15) would

2 a. since b. for c. for d. for e. since f. for g. for h. for

3 a. How long have they been in London? – Since 1974, I think. b. How long has he been in the office? – Since he arrived here an hour ago, I think. c. How long has the chief engineer been in the research department? – Since four o'clock this afternoon, I think. d. How long has she been in Hamburg? – Since January 1975, I think. e. How long has he been in Hull? – Since last Monday, I think.

4 a. I've had the motor bike for six weeks now. b. She's known John for two years now. c. They've been in Germany for two days now. d. He's been here for half an hour now. e. I've known Fred for three months now. f. She's had the new car for four weeks now.

5 a. what b. which c. what d. who e. Which

6 a. I haven't seen Fred for a week (now). b. How long have you been here (now)? – For about four weeks. c. How long have you known Mr Baldinger (now)? – For a year, I think. d. How long has Fred had the car (now)? – Oh, he's had it for at least three years (now). e. How long has he been in the workshop (now)? – Since this morning. f. We've been in London for four days (now).

LESSON 6

Zusätzliche Informationen

What's new on the market?

Aus einer Originalanzeige der *Precision Screw & MFG. Company:*

Nyltite fasteners are screws or bolts fitted with a scientifically designed nylon locking seal, which flows inwards when the fastener is tightened. The perfect locking seal. Resists vibration, seals against air, water, oils, most chemicals and electrolytic corrosion. The ultimate economy. Nyltite fasteners provide the lowest installed cost of all sealing and locking fasteners. Available to suit screws of all sizes in general use. Try Nyltite locking seals on your screws. Also available in small kits of assorted sizes for you to assess them thoroughly.

Text- und Transferfragen

The meeting ...

Who has called a meeting?
Does the meeting take place in England or in Germany?
What's the main subject of the discussion?
Do you remember some of the advantages of monorail conveyors?
What are the track sections made of?
Are the monorail conveyors supplied in metric sizes, too?
Can the company supply on time?
Is it very important to be able to supply on time?
(Why? Why not?)
Do English companies usually supply on time? What about German companies? American companies?
Do you think it's necessary to have leaflets in German for the German customers? (Why? Why not?)

What's new on the market?
How are Nyltite seals used?
Why are they used?
Can you say something about their strength?

Methodische Hinweise und Schlüssel

1 a. No, they haven't. I've been waiting for them since last Monday. **b.** No, she hasn't. I've been waiting for her since early this morning. **c.** No, they haven't. I've been waiting for them since eight o'clock this morning. **d.** No, they haven't. I've been waiting for them for over a week (now). **e.** No, it hasn't. I've been waiting for it for three weeks (now). **f.** No, they haven't. I've been waiting for them since last Wednesday.

2 "Were you in Germany last week?"
"Yes, I *was.*"
"Did you see Mr Baldinger, too?"
"Oh yes, of course I *did.*"
"Is he interested in our new range of conveyors?"
"Well, yes, I think he *is.*"
"Did you explain the conveyors to him?"
"Yes, I *did.*"
"What did he say? Can he sell our conveyors in Germany?"
"Well, yes, he said he *could.*"
"Did you give him our leaflets?"
"Yes, I *did.*"
"Did he like them?"
"No, he *didn't.*"
"Why not?"
"He said he needed leaflets in German for his German customers."

3 Freie schriftliche Übung ohne Schlüssel. Auf formale Genauigkeit sollte in diesem Stadium noch nicht viel Wert gelegt werden. Es genügt vollständig, wenn der Kursteilnehmer in der Lage ist, einen allgemein verständlichen kurzen Bericht zu schreiben (in verhältnismäßig einfacher Sprache).

4 a. What Fred needs is a new motor bike. **b.** What John needs is a holiday in England. **c.** What the company needs is a new chief engineer. **d.** What we need is a representative in Germany. **e.** What they need are some new ideas. **f.** What we need are Nyltite seals. **g.** What the technician needs is a new tool kit.

5 a. in **b.** on **c.** in ... on **d.** in

6 a. I've been waiting for the chief engineer for half an hour (now). **b.** How long have you been living in Hamburg (now)? – For about two years. **c.** Mr Baldinger has been a representative of an English firm for a month (now). **d.** Fred has been in the workshop since this morning.

7 a. Who is the company's chief engineer? **b.** Do you know the name of the German representative? **c.** What can you tell me about floor space? **d.** Can the conveyor handle heavy loads? **e.** Is it possible to build the conveyor in any length? **f.** What are the sections made of? **g.** Are the sections supplied in standard lengths? **h.** How are the conveyors assembled? **i.** Can the conveyors be supplied on time? **j.** Why haven't they got any leaflets in German?

32

k. Do you think it's easier to sell something in Germany when you have leaflets in German? **l.** Would you like to be the company's representative in Germany?

LESSON 7

Zusätzliche Informationen

... and the minutes

the Continent: "the mainland of Europe, as distinguished from the British Isles"

What's new on the market?

Als Hintergrundinformation hier der vollständige Text des Kurzartikels aus der Fachzeitschrift *Design Engineering* (Morgan-Grampian Ltd, 30 Calderwood Street, Woolwich, London SE18 6QH):

Absorption bumper cuts cost of accidents

To minimise the injuries inflicted on the passengers in a car crash, the rate of deceleration of the car must be reduced to as low a level as possible. Most modern cars now have front and rear body sections designed to collapse progressively. But now Imperial Metal Industries has developed a bumper which absorbs energy by squeezing a plastic cartridge through a suitable aperture.

The basic structural features of the vehicle bumper are shown in Figure 1 *(= Abbildung im Lehrbuch)*, which illustrates the initial movement of the device after impact. The ram (the left-hand end is attached to the bumper) moves to the right, and plastic material is extruded from the annular die forming the mouth of the container. Legislation will require the system to be recoverable and in this design, the recovery and extrusion phases follow in sequence.

During a low-speed impact (up to 5 mile/h) the plastic cartridge deforms in a barrelling mode and subsequently recovers its shape. At higher impact speeds, the cartridge is extruded through the mouth of the container to absorb large amounts of kinetic energy by deformation and displacement.

At the design stage, it is possible to tailor impact-absorption devices to suit the specific impact levels, decelerations, and displacements which may be specified by vehicle designers or road safety legislators. Performance variations, based on technical data already amassed, are achieved by the alteration of various parameters including cartridge formulation and pre-treatment, and the judicious choice of extrusion ratio and die geometry.

Text- und Transferfragen

... and the minutes

Can you explain what "minutes" are?
What are these minutes about?
What sort of information should be given in minutes?
(date, place, participants, subject, etc.)

What's new on the market?
What are the main features of the new bumper?
How does it work?
Can the new bumper help prevent damage during a *high-speed* impact?
Do you think this bumper is a good idea? (Why? Why not?)

Methodische Hinweise und Schlüssel

1 a. No, they said they couldn't supply on time. **b.** No, they said they weren't interested in monorail conveyors. **c.** No, they said they didn't want to open an office in Germany. **d.** No, they said they weren't going to have a meeting next week. **e.** No, they said they hadn't used plastic material. **f.** No, they said they hadn't solved the problem. **g.** No, they said they hadn't talked to Mr Baldinger. **h.** No, they said they wouldn't sell their products in America.

2 a. He assured them that the plastic material would be sent very soon. **b.** She assured him that the operating manual would be ready very soon. **c.** We assured her that the car would be repaired very soon. **d.** They assured us that the steel sections would be delivered very soon. **e.** We assured them that the problem would be discussed very soon. **f.** She assured them that the batteries would be checked very soon.

3 Methodisch wäre folgendes Verfahren denkbar:

Teilnehmer 1: "'Did you have a pleasant flight?' Mr Jasper wanted to know."
Teilnehmer 2: "Sorry, what did he want to know?"
Teilnehmer 1: "He wanted to know whether I had had a pleasant flight."
Teilnehmer 1: "'Well, I'm very glad to see you', Mr Lawrence said."
Teilnehmer 2: "Sorry, what did he say?"
Teilnehmer 1: "He said he was very glad to see me."

b. Mr Lawrence said that he was very glad to see me. **c.** Mr Mills asked whether we should discuss the monorail conveyors. **d.** Mr Lawrence asked whether I knew the advantages of their system. **e.** Mr Mills wanted to know whether I wanted them in metric sizes. **f.** Mr Jasper pointed out that the sections were made of cold-rolled steel. **g.** Mr Lawrence said (that) they had very good leaflets. **h.** Mr. Mills said that they could supply on time. **i.** Mr Mills wanted to know whether I thought that leaflets in German were necessary. **j.** Mr L awrence said that most Germans spoke English.

34

4 **b.** Well, he said they could. **c.** Well, he said they were. **d.** Well, he said they did. **e.** Well, he said it was. **f.** Well, he said they could. **g.** Well, he said they would. **h.** Well, he said they had. **i.** Well, he said they did. **j.** Well, he said they were.

LESSON 8

Zusätzliche Informationen

The hovercraft principle

hovercraft: "A craft which can hover over or move across water or land surface while being held off the surfaces by a cushion of air. The cushion is produced either by pumping air into a plenum chamber *(= Speicherraum)* under the craft or by ejecting air downwards and inwards through a peripheral ring of nozzles. Propulsion can be by tilting the craft, or by jet, or air propellor, or, over water, by water propellor, or, over land, by low-pressure tyres or tracks."

hydrofoil: "A fast, light craft fitted with wing-like structures (foils) on struts under the hull. These may be extendable and adjustable. Propelled by propellor in water or air, or by jet. Foils may act entirely or partly submerged with hull lifted clear of the water at speed."

(Hovercraft [= Luftkissenboot] und hydrofoil [= Gleitkufenboot] sind also zwei grundverschiedene Konzepte!

craft: 1 skill or dexterity *(= Fertigkeit; Geschicklichkeit)*; 2 a trade or occupation requiring manual skill *(= Handwerk; Gewerbe;* craftsman = *Handwerker)*; 3 ships or vessels collectively; 4 a single ship or vessel; 5 aircraft collectively; 6 a single aircraft

Verwendung der Luftkissenboote: Nicht nur als Kanalfähre, sondern auch als "cable-layer, ice-breakers, . . . coastal defence vessels, missile-carriers and submarine-killers" werden *hovercraft* eingesetzt. In einem Artikel, der am 14. Juli 1976 in der englischen Zeitschrift *Weekend* erschien, heißt es weiter:

The sleek Arab dhow *(= Dau [arabischer Schiffstyp])* was speeding through the night, making one of its regular smuggling runs from the Arabian coast to India with a cargo of contraband gold, when an ear-shattering roar and cloud of spray came over the horizon. The smugglers watched, stunned, as a hovercraft raced up to them at 50 knots, and customs men boarded the dhow and seized the gold. It was the first time the Arabs had seen one of these craft. In a few weeks about 300 smugglers were intercepted by a single SR.N6 hovercraft, chartered by the Indian Government. From one dhow gold worth £200,000 was recovered. The smuggling trade was smashed.

Quellen für zusätzliches Arbeitsmaterial: British Hovercraft Corporation, East Cowes, Isle of Wight; Zeitschrift: *Hovering Craft and Hydrofoil,* 51 Welbeck Street, London W1.

A simple experiment

"The iron filings will arrange themselves in circles round the wire when the current is flowing."

Text- und	Can you explain how hovercraft work?
Transferfragen	Have you ever seen a hovercraft? (Where?)
	What can hovercraft be used for?
	What are the main advantages of hovercraft?

Methodische Hinweise und Schlüssel

1 a. wrong **b.** right **c.** right **d.** wrong **e.** right **f.** wrong **g.** wrong

2 a. Could you check the battery if you had some instruments? – The battery? No, I'm sure I couldn't. **b.** Could you operate the hovercraft if you had an operating manual? – The hovercraft? No, I'm sure I couldn't. **c.** Could you design the turbine if you had a computer? – The turbine? No, I'm sure I couldn't. **d.** Could you carry out the experiment if you had enough material? – The experiment? No, I'm sure I couldn't. **e.** Could you assemble the loudspeaker if you had enough time? – The loudspeaker? No, I'm sure I couldn't.

3 a. were **b.** no ... not **c.** are **d.** more **e.** speeds

4 a. Can you explain the hovercraft principle? *(Hier jeweils Antwort des Teilnehmers!)* **b.** What do you know about the early hovercraft? **c.** Have you ever travelled by hovercraft? **d.** What is the function of the flexible skirt? **e.** Have you ever carried out an experiment like the one shown in this lesson? **f.** Do you think such experiments are interesting?

5 a. The first hovercraft used a simple chamber. **b.** Through this chamber air was fed to form an air cushion under the craft. **c.** The first hovercraft were driven by piston engines. **d.** Today, lighter, more powerful gas turbines are used to drive the lift fan and the propulsion propellor (through a transmission system). **e.** British Rail Hovercraft Ltd. (one of the two companies that use hovercraft) cross the English Channel. **f.** British Rail Hovercraft Ltd. take you (and your car) from Calais to Dover in about 35 minutes. **g.** Although the crossing of the Channel (from Calais to Dover) takes only about 35 minutes, there is still enough time to get sick if the sea is rough. **h.** For this experiment use a length of 25 cm of copper wire and put it through the hole in a piece of white cardboard. **i.** You must connect the ends to the plus and minus terminals of the low-voltage supply. **j.** You must sprinkle some iron filings on the cardboard. **k.** You must put the copper wire through the hole in a piece of white cardboard. – Sprinkle some iron filings on the cardboard. – Switch on the current, and tap the cardboard lightly with a pencil. **l.** You must tap the cardboard lightly with a pencil.

6 a. the ... – **b.** – **c.** –

7 a. Since we didn't have any time, we couldn't talk with (*oder:* to) the chief engineer. **b.** Could you send us two batteries next week? **c.** Yesterday a representative was here who was able to explain everything to us. **d.** I don't know if we'll be able to drive (*oder:* travel) to Birmingham next week. **e.** It would be very nice if you could send us the new leaflets (*oder:* brochures) soon. **f.** When I asked him yesterday evening he told me he couldn't repair the machine.

LESSON 9

Zusätzliche Informationen

Wie schon in Lektion 4, so wird auch hier wieder amerikanisches Englisch vorgestellt, sowohl vom Wortschatz her als auch hinsichtlich der Aussprache (vgl. Sprecher auf den Tonmaterialien).

Was eine allgemeine Einführung in das amerikanische Englisch angeht, so wird auf die Erläuterungen in Lektion 4 verwiesen.

store [stɔ:r] *Br.:* shop	**parking lot** – *Br.:* car park
truck – *Br.:* lorry	**salesman** – *Br.:* commercial traveller
trucker – *Br.:* lorry driver	

Text- und Transferfragen

What is this text about?
Who uses CB radios?
How much is an average CB radio?
What does "Smokey" mean?
What is a "hit-and-run-driver"?
Who was killed by a hit-and-run driver?
How was the driver caught?
How can you find a good restaurant along the highway?
Do you need a license to operate a CB radio?

Which of the truckers' slang expressions do you remember?
Do you think CB radios would be useful in Germany, too?
Would you like to have one? (What for?)

Methodische Hinweise und Schlüssel

1 A1+B4 / A2+B1 / A3+B2 / A4+B5 / A5+B3

2 a. He was the manager of a radio store, I think. **b.** He called the police,
I think. **c.** He bought a CB radio last week, I think. **d.** He was from Pasadena, I think.

3 Die Teilnehmer sollten in diesem Stadium des Lernens angehalten werden,
schriftliche Übungen wie die vorliegende möglichst frei durchzuführen, d. h.
ohne die Hilfe des Textes.
Wenn die Durchführung einer solchen schriftlichen Übung im Unterricht nicht
möglich ist, kann man sie als Hausaufgabe vorsehen.

4 a. radio (*oder:* CB radio) **b.** picture taker **c.** highway **d.** emergency
e. channel **f.** Smokey (the bear) **g.** trucker (*Br.:* lorry driver) **h.** feed the
bears

5 a. What do you think about CB radios? (Hier natürlich jeweils Antwort der
Teilnehmer.) **b.** Have you ever seen such a radio? **c.** How much do CB
radios cost in the USA? **d.** How much is this in German money? **e.** Can you
tell me what CB radios are used for? **f.** What does "Smokey" mean? **g.** Why
do truckers look out for antennas in the parking lots of restaurants? **h.** What
does "FCC" mean?

LESSON 10

Zusätzliche Informationen

Die internationale Gesellschaft Airbus Industrie (37 Bd. de Montmorency,
Paris 16e) vergab Teilaufträge für den Airbus an folgende Firmen:

S. N. I. Aerospatiale (Frankreich):	Fuselage nose section
	Wing/fuselage centre section
Deutsche Airbus:	Remainder of fuselage
	Empennage ['empinidz] (= Leitwerk)
Hawker Siddeley (Großbritannien):	Wing box
Fokker (Niederlande):	Wing moving surfaces

Diese vier Firmen verfügen insgesamt über mehr als 130,000 Arbeitskräfte.
Zur Veranschaulichung der Inneneinrichtung des Airbus (und eventuell zum
Einsatz im Unterricht, wenn zusätzlicher Stoff verkraftet werden kann) hier
noch einige Zeilen aus der Airbusbroschüre:

As with the new generation aircraft to be introduced on medium- and long-haul routes in the 1970s, the A300B has a more comfortable and spacious cabin than current aircraft.

Passenger seating is six, seven or eight abreast, all with two aisles (= *Gang*), in first-class, coach-class and tourist-class arrangements. In all these layouts no passenger is more than one place away from an aisle. This contrasts favourably with the six-abreast seating in current aircraft or the nine- and ten-abreast arrangements in new wider-fuselage aircraft, all of which have triple seats. Each passenger has ample stowage space for coats and hand baggage.

The proportions of the A300B passenger cabin give great flexibility in the choice of layout. In the European market eight-abreast configuration give seating comfort comparable to current aircraft but with a much greater sense of spaciousness, while a seven-abreast layout is well suited to the North American market.

Typical mixed class layouts seat 200 to 240 passengers six, seven or eight abreast, while over 300 can be accommodated in a single class arrangement. Twin aisles run the whole length of the cabin, allowing faster loading of passengers and easier movement for cabin staff.

module: "an assembly within a geometrical framework of electronic units functioning as a system"

module technique: (= Modultechnik: das Zusammenfassen von Bauteilen in einer Einheit, erleichtert die Montage und den Service)

Text- und Transferfragen

The A300B – a European aircraft
Who built the Airbus?
Where was it built?
Is it used by the airlines?
What do you remember about the engines?
Have you ever seen an Airbus?
Have you ever travelled by plane? Which plane did you use?
What do you think is the "best" plane?
Which airline do you think is the safest?
Have you ever been on a charter plane? Do you think charter planes are as safe as other planes?

Any questions?
What is "aquaplaning"?
Have you ever had trouble with it?
What can you do to prevent aquaplaning?

Can you explain what a breathalyser is?
When is it used?
Have the police ever asked you to blow into a breathalyser?
What do you think about "drinking and driving"?

Methodische Hinweise und Schlüssel

1 a. Well, the technician I asked couldn't help me at all. **b.** Well, the chief engineer I discussed it with didn't know anything at all. **c.** Well, the girl I explained it to wasn't interested at all. **d.** Well, the representative I saw in Germany didn't like them at all. **e.** Well, the trucker I met in the restaurant wasn't interested at all.

2 a. But they're not the iron filings I need in the factory! **b.** But they're not the leaflets I mentioned at the meeting! **c.** But they're not the tools I ordered! **d.** But they're not the drills I saw in the workshop! **e.** But they're not the CB radios I spoke about!

3 a. I'm thinking of the new leaflets I ordered last week. **b.** I'm writing to the girl I saw in the office. **c.** He was talking about the APU unit he installed last month. **d.** He's explaining it to the technician he phoned this morning. **e.** They're talking about the new computer they bought some weeks ago.

4 Wenn die Lücken ausgefüllt sind, sollte diese Übung auch mündlich (z. B. Teilnehmer 1 / Teilnehmer 2) durchgeführt werden.
a. Where do you live? – I live in London. – Oh, do you? How long have you been living in London? – For about a year or so, I think. **b.** Where did you live before you went to London? – In Hamburg. – Oh, did you? How long did you live in Hamburg? – For about two years, I think. – **c.** Where do you work? – I work in a car factory. – Oh, do you? How long have you been working in a car factory? – Since October last year, I think. **d.** What did you do when you were in Hamburg? – I made technical drawings. – Oh, did you? How long did you make technical drawings? — For about eighteen months, I think. **e.** What are you doing at the moment? – I'm working with the computer. – Oh, are you? How long have you been working with the computer? – Since last week, I think. **f.** And what did you do before that? – I worked in the office. – Oh, did you? How long did you work in the office? – For about a month, I think. **g.** What hobbies are you interested in? – I'm interested in model airplanes. – Oh, are you? How long have you been interested in model airplanes? – Since I was a child, I think.

TEST A

Es wurde versucht, auf knappem Raum eine möglichst große Vielzahl von Test-Items unterzubringen, damit ein einigermaßen verläßliches Ergebnis zustande kommt.

Trotzdem kann ein solcher Test nicht alles abdecken, besonders nicht die mündlichen Fertigkeiten. Es ist also empfehlenswert, diesen Test durch eine mündliche Prüfung zu ergänzen, auch wenn sie nur kurz sein kann. Diese mündliche Komponente kann vom einfachen Vorlesen eines Textes bis zum mündlichen Verständnistest reichen (etwa in der Form, wie er in TEST C durchgeführt wird).

TEST A hat den Vorteil, daß man ihn schnell und ohne große Mühe durchführen kann. Er besteht insgesamt aus 70 Items, die sich mit Wortschatz und Strukturen (Grammatik), Aussprache, Rechtschreibung, Betonung und Übersetzung befassen. Der Übersetzungstest dient nicht der Prüfung der besonderen Fertigkeit „Übersetzen" (die ja viel mehr umfaßt), sondern ganz einfach dem Abtesten einiger wichtiger Strukturen und Vokabeln.

Ein Kursteilnehmer sollte etwa 40 der 70 Items richtig gelöst haben, wenn man von einem ausreichenden Ergebnis sprechen will. Wegen der Vielfalt der Kurse und Lehrgänge bleibt es dem Kursleiter überlassen, ein ihm geeignet erscheinendes Bewertungsschema aufzustellen, wenn das erforderlich sein sollte.

Schlüssel zu den Items

1–13: Wortschatz und Strukturen

1c 2b 3d 4a 5b 6c 7a 8d 9a 10b 11b 12c 13c

14–20: Aussprache

14d 15b 16a 17b 18a 19a 20b

21–40: Rechtschreibung

(Die folgenden Sätze sollten vom Kursleiter in normalem Sprechtempo vorgelesen werden, und zwar am besten zweimal. Der Kursteilnehmer schreibt das jeweils fehlende Wort in die Lücken oder auf ein separates Blatt Papier:)

21 Both engines make use of modern <u>module</u> construction techniques.
22 The <u>auxiliary</u> power unit of the A300B makes the aircraft independent of ground power sources.
23 The Condeep platform consists of <u>cylindrical</u> cells, 185 feet high.

24 After constructing the base, it is <u>floated</u> out to a deep water site.

25 The chief engineer said it was very easy to assemble the <u>various</u> parts.

26 Some of the brain-storming sessions I attended were <u>leisurely</u> discussions, others desperate ones looking for urgent improvement.

27 Must the device be <u>weatherproof</u>?

28 "Hi-fi" is the <u>abbreviation</u> for "high fidelity".

29 Do you know how to <u>measure</u> resistance?

30 I'd like to discuss our new range of <u>conveyors</u> with you.

31 I'm sure our customers would prefer <u>publicity</u> material in German.

32 On impact, plastic material is <u>extruded</u> from the two devices, thus absorbing large amounts of energy.

33 The skirts – flexible <u>curtains</u> fitted below the bottom edges – also act as shock absorbers.

34 You can use an <u>accumulator</u> for this experiment.

35 Two of the supporting <u>columns</u> can be used for drilling.

36 The microwave energy is confined within the food <u>cavity</u>.

37 The <u>tensile</u> strength of the new seals is 15,000 lb/in².

38 A Dolby system reduces noise without <u>affecting</u> the original quality.

39 I think we should use <u>reinforced</u> concrete for this project.

40 You'll get some information about <u>soldering</u>, too.

41–51: Wortschatz und Strukturen

41b 42a 43c 44b 45b 46a 47d 48d 49c 50d 51a

52–61: Betonung

52 al | <u>ter</u> | na | tive 53 a | <u>pol</u> | o | gy 54 <u>a</u> | qua | plan | ing 55 aux | <u>il</u> | ia | ry
56 com | mu | ni | <u>ca</u> | tions 57 e | <u>mer</u> | gen | cy 58 <u>hel</u> | i | cop | ters
59 con | <u>sist</u> | ing 60 mod | u | <u>la</u> | tion 61 <u>sub</u> | se | quent

62–70: Übersetzung

(62) Yesterday I read that Lufthansa (has) bought the airbus. (63) Do you know why they decided on that plane? (64) The decision is said to have been easy since the airbus is the only plane that has been specially designed for short- and medium-haul service. (65) But other airlines haven't bought the airbus yet, have they? (66) As far as I know, five or six airlines have bought it already. (67) And who are the engines from? (68) Well, I think two alternatives are offered by the manufacturers: first the Rolls-Royce RB211–22, and secondly the General Electric CF6–50A. (69) Are both engines equally powerful? (70) No, I think the General Electric engine is a little more powerful.

Zusätzliche Informationen

A simple experiment

Erläuterungen zum Experiment: "When the air is removed from the tube, the coin and the paper fall, and surprisingly they reach the bottom of the tube at the same time, as did the two balls . . . The air was rubbing against the light piece of paper and the friction force produced partly balanced out the effect of the force of gravity . . ."

Text- und Transferfragen

Stirling Moss tests your dream car
What does Stirling Moss say about the old Jaguar E-type?
Have you ever driven a Jaguar E-type?
What is the name of its successor?
What does Stirling Moss say about the styling of the new car?
Have you ever seen it?
What does Stirling Moss criticize about the new model?
Do you remember how much the XJ-S costs?
How much is this in German money?
Do you like sports cars?
Do you know any other cars that could be called "best-sellers"?

A simple experiment
What do you need for this experiment?
What will happen when you repeat the experiment after pumping out the air?

Methodische Hinweise und Schlüssel

1 a. I don't know which engineer she means. **b.** I don't know which leaflets they ordered. **c.** I don't know which car she'll buy. **d.** I don't know which tuner he's interested in. **e.** I don't know which report they discussed. **f.** I don't know which engine she oiled.

2 a. m . . . in(s) **b.** mph **c.** lb(s) **d.** m^2

3 a. until **b.** although **c.** whether **d.** After **e.** because **f.** than

4 Für freie Kommunikationsübungen dieser Art werden von nun an keine

Lösungen mehr vorgegeben, da mit steigenden Fertigkeiten auch die Variationsmöglichkeiten größer werden und sich nicht mehr in ein Schema pressen lassen.

5 Siehe Übung 4.

LESSON 12

Zusätzliche Informationen

Als Hintergrundinformation einige Passagen aus einer Broschüre, die vom *Electricity Board* herausgegeben wird:

Electric melting offers valuable benefits — both technical and economic — to this industry. Future growth in this competitive field undoubtedly relies on achieving higher production volume by investment in high-speed automated foundry plant. Induction melting is making an invaluable contribution to the modernisation of aluminium diecasting foundries *(= Druckgießereien)* — notably in the form of channel furnaces, which are used widely for both melting and holding, particularly for long runs of the same alloy in multi-shift operations, and coreless furnaces which are used to great advantage by foundries producing wide ranges of alloys.

Why induction melting...
It is recognised that the *quality* of metal from an electric furnace is higher than that from any fuelfired melter; and, when the *overall* cost of melting is considered, electric melting is just as economic.
Improved product quality — due to better compositional control, freedom from gas pick-up (no combustion products!), reduced alloy losses (more accurate temperature control). In short, more productivity because of fewer rejects.
Economic melting — due to rapid heating (big throughputs *(= Durchsatz, Leistung)* from a relatively small furnace), lower operating costs (longer crucible/lining life), lower melting losses than any other melting method, efficient melting of returns, efficient heating (all the heat goes into the charge), minimum maintenance requirements, reduced need for quality control and inspection...

...and induction holding?
Many of the above benefits apply equally to electric *holding* furnaces *(= Wärmöfen, Warmhalteöfen, Abstehöfen)*. The precise temperature control which characterises electric furnaces is especially important — to avoid losing the more volatile constituents, to minimise grain growth and to avoid sludge formation. Minimal oxidation and freedom from gas pick-up are also important, enabling high-quality metal to be consistently achieved. *Furthermore, electric holding can be fully automated, with no need for a skilled operator in attendance.*

Electric furnaces in action
For diecasting foundries the route to increased profitability lies with higher throughputs and the optimum use of labour — which implies a much higher degree of automation. Electric melting and holding are making increasingly important contributions to the prosperity of the industry. Here are just two examples which show how electric furnaces can provide the highest quality metal, efficiently and reliably, to satisfy the most demanding production requirements.

44

induction furnace: "application of induction heating in which the metal to be melted forms the secondary *(= Sekundärwicklung)* of a transformer"

induction heating: "that arising from eddy currents *(= Wirbelströme)* in conducting material, e.g. solder, profiles of gear-wheels, conductor coils around vessels for heating liquids, etc.; generated with a high-frequency source, usually oscillators of high power, operating at 10^6–10^7 Hz"

coreless induction furnace: "a high-frequency induction furnace in which there is no iron magnetic circuit other than the charge in the furnace itself"

Text- und **Transferfragen**	Where does the conversation take place? What does Mr Reed say about the use of electric furnaces? What is the basic principle of an arc furnace? Do all induction furnaces work on the same basic principle? Have you ever seen an induction furnace? (If yes, where and when?)

Methodische Hinweise und Schlüssel

1 a. Well, I wonder if they really have. **b.** Well, I wonder if she really does. **c.** Well, I wonder if he really is. **d.** Well, I wonder if she really has. **e.** Well, I wonder if he really does. **f.** Well, I wonder if she really has.

2 b. Well, that depends on the machines we're going to buy. **c.** Well, that depends on the number of workers we're going to hire. **d.** Well, that depends on the calculations we're going to make. **e.** Well, that depends on the number of products we're going to sell.

3 a. The electric motor is being oiled at the moment. **b.** The English letters are being translated at the moment. **c.** The body is being painted at the moment. **d.** The experiment is being carried out at the moment. **e.** The aluminium windows are being installed at the moment. **f.** The spindle is being repaired at the moment. **g.** The components are being measured at the moment. **h.** The manifold is being cleaned at the moment. **i.** The leaflets are being prepared at the moment. **j.** The computer is being programmed at the moment. **k.** The machine parts are being welded at the moment.

4 a. wrong **b.** wrong **c.** right **d.** right **e.** right

5 a. on . . . in **b.** in . . . in **c.** on

6 a. Have you already repaired my car? – No, but it's being repaired at the moment. **b.** Do these furnaces offer any advantages? – Well, that depends on the type of metal you want to use. **c.** Were you in the factory yesterday, too? – Yes. It was very interesting, wasn't it? **d.** Is the new Jaguar heavier than the old one? – I don't know, but it looks heavier.

7 Freie Kommunikationsübung, daher kein Schlüssel. Je nach Unterrichtssituation ergeben sich aus diesen Übungen oft Gespräche, die man leicht ausbauen kann. Z. B. die Frage *Have you ever visited a factory?* kann leicht zu einem Gespräch über die Fabriken der Heimatstadt verwendet werden *(What are the main factories in your town? Have you ever visited any of them? How many people work there? Where are the products sold? etc.)*

LESSON 13

Zusätzliche Informationen

Dieser Text basiert auf einem Tatsachenbericht in der englischen Wochenzeitschrift *Weekend*.

Text- und Transferfragen Where did the accident happen?
What did the Australian managers think about the box-girder system used for this bridge?
What was wrong with two of the metal spans?
What did they do to change this?
What happened then?
Where was John Hindshaw when the accident happened?
How many people were killed in the accident?
Have you ever heard about similar accidents? (If yes, where? When? What happened?)
Why do you think such accidents happen?
What can be done to prevent them?

Methodische Hinweise und Schlüssel

1 b. He suggested that we should stop working and call the technician. **c.** He suggested that we should wait for the technicians. **d.** He suggested that we should start with the motor. **e.** He suggested that we should tell him about the trouble we had.

2 a. It had already been tuned when I got there. **b.** They had already been installed when I got there. **c.** It had already been discussed when I got there.

d. They had already been written when I got there. **e.** It had already been carried out when I got there. **f.** They had already been replaced when I got there. **g.** They had already been welded when I got there. **h.** They had already been assembled when I got there. **i.** It had already been sold when I got there. **j.** It had already been painted when I got there. **k.** They had already been repaired when I got there. **l.** They had already been worked out when I got there.

3 Freie schriftliche Übung (z. B. als Hausarbeit), daher keine Lösungsvorschläge.

4 a. Our monorail conveyor system was a great success from the moment it was introduced in 1976. **b.** Our air conditioning units were a great success from the moment they were introduced last December. **c.** Our sophisticated electronic equipment was a great success from the moment it was introduced in 1975. **d.** Our single-lens reflex cameras were a great success from the moment they were introduced two years ago. **e.** Our sprinkler units were a great success from the moment they were introduced six months ago.

5 a. As far as I know he did. **b.** As far as I know he does. **c.** As far as I know they do. **d.** As far as I know he would. **e.** As far as I know they will.

6 a. — **b.** the **c.** the . . . — **d.** the . . . the **e.** the . . . the

LESSON 14

Zusätzliche Informationen

The funny side of electronics (I)

Diese Lektion ist wieder dem amerikanischen Englisch gewidmet, hauptsächlich jedoch hinsichtlich der Sprecher auf den Tonmaterialien. An lexikalischen Amerikanismen findet man nur

I guess = Br.: **I suppose, I assume** (*guess* im britischen Englisch = raten, erraten).

Alle anderen Ausdrücke sind auch im britischen Englisch gebräuchlich.

Im übrigen sei auf die Ausführungen in Lektion 4 verwiesen.

Any questions?

aluminium (*US:* aluminum [əˈluːmənəm]): "silver-white metallic element, forming a protective film of oxide; symbol Al; obtained from bauxite, it has numerous uses and is the basis of light alloys for use in, e.g., structural work; alloyed with silicon (['silikən]: *Silizium*) for transformer laminations, and iron and cobalt in many types of permanent magnet"

brass: "primarily, name applied to an alloy of copper and zinc, but other elements such as aluminium, iron, manganese, nickel, tin, and lead are frequently added"

copper: "bright, reddish metallic element, symbol Cu; it often occurs in thin sheets of plates, filling narrow cracks or fissures; copper is ductile, with high electrical and thermal conductivity, good resistance to corrosion; basis of bronze, brass, aluminium bronze, and other alloys"

lead: "a metallic element, symbol Pb; the metal is bluish-grey, the densest and softest of the common metals; on account of its resistance to corrosion, extensively used for roofing, cable sheathing, and for lining apparatus in the chemical industry; it is used as shielding in X-ray and nuclear work because of its relative cheapness, high density, and nuclear properties; other principal uses: in storage batteries, sound absorbers, ammunition, foil, and as a constituent of bearing metals, solder, and type-metal; lead can be hardened by the addition of arsenic or antimony"

mercury: "a white metallic element which is liquid* at atmospheric temperature; symbol Hg; a solvent for most metals, the products being called amalgams *(= Amalgam);* its chief uses are in the manufacture of drugs and chemicals, fulminates *(fulminate of mercury = Knallquecksilber),* and vermilion *(= Zinnoberrot);* used as metal in mercury-vapour lamps, power-control switches, and in many scientific and electrical instruments; also called quicksilver"

platinum: "a metallic element, symbol Pt; platinum is the most important of a group of six closely related rare metals, the others being osmium, iridium, palladium, rhodium, and ruthenium; it is heavy, soft, and ductile, immune to attack by most chemical reagents and to oxidation at high temperatures; used for making jewellery, special scientific apparatus, electrical contacts for high temperatures and for electrodes subjected to possible chemical attack; also used as a basic metal for resistance thermometry over a wide temperature range"

silver: "a pure white metallic element, symbol Ag; the metal is not oxidized in air; the best electrical conductor and the main constituent of photographic emulsions; used for ornaments, mirrors, cutlery, jewellery, etc., and for certain

---

* **liquids:** "substances such as water, oil, alcohol, and the like, that are neither solids nor gases"
fluids: "anything that flows, whether liquid or gaseous"

components in food and chemical industry where cheaper metals fail to withstand corrosion"

tin: "a soft, silvery-white metallic element, ductile and malleable *(= streckbar, hämmerbar);* symbol Sn; not affected by air or water at ordinary temperatures; the principal use is as a coating on steel in tin-plate *(= Zinkblech, Weißblech);* also used as a constituent in alloys and with lead in low-melting point solders for electrical connections"

electrolyte: "chemical, or its solution in water, which conducts current through ionization"

Text- und Transferfragen	**The funny side of electronics (I)**

The funny side of electronics (I)
Where were the two passengers?
What were they talking about?
What was announced over the loudspeaker?
Do you think it will be possible in the near future to make tourist trips to the moon?
Would you like to go to the moon?
Do you think it will be possible for such a trip to be fully automatic? (Why not?)

Any questions?
Can you give me some examples of metals that are good conductors?
What are good conductors needed for?
What change is there in conductivity when temperature rises?

Methodische Hinweise und Schlüssel

1 Freie Kommunikationsübung ohne Schlüssel. Als zusätzliche Übung kann man die Story auch von zwei oder drei Kursteilnehmern nacherzählen lassen bzw. eine solche Nacherzählung als Wiederholungsübung in der folgenden Stunde machen lassen.

2 a. I don't mind talking to the chief engineer. **b.** I don't mind checking the engines. **c.** I don't mind installing the computer. **d.** I don't mind working in the workshop for a couple of days. **e.** I don't mind using the computer.

3 a. at . . . a . . . in **b.** be . . . for **c.** a

4 a. Well, I'd rather have an operating manual. **b.** Well, I'd rather go to Pittsburgh. **c.** Well, I'd rather work in Germany. **d.** Well, I'd rather repair the engine. **e.** Well, I'd rather fly to the USA.

5 a. Lead **b.** Aluminium (*US:* Aluminum) **c.** silver **d.** Copper **e.** gold
f. Platinum **g.** steel **h.** iron **i.** mercury

LESSON 15

Zusätzliche Informationen

A calculator that talks to you

Hier noch ein paar Angaben aus der Originalbroschüre:

The SPEECH PLUS calculator

◾ verifies all keystrokes and answers with 24 words from earphone or self-contained speaker;

◾ is hand-held, rechargeable, portable;

◾ uses a keyboard with layout and keys selected for maximum accuracy during non-visual operation.

constant: "in an algebraic expression or equation, a quantity (or parameter) which remains the same while the variables change; π is an absolute constant"

What's new on the market?

epoxy (or epoxide) resins ['rezinz] *(= Harze):* "polymers, widely used as structural plastics, surface coatings and adhesives, and for encapsulating and embedding electronic components; characterized by low shrinkage on polymerization, good adhesion, mechanical and electrical strength, and chemical resistance"

**Text- und
Transferfragen**

A calculator that talks to you
What is unusual about the new calculator?
Who is it particularly useful for?

What's new on the market?
What are the strongest adhesives?
What are they used for?
How are they normally used?
What has been developed by the English company?
Do you think this is a good idea?

Methodische Hinweise und Schlüssel

1 Freie Kommunikationsübung, daher ohne Schlüssel

2 Siehe **1.**

3 a. No, an adhesive won't do, I'm afraid. **b.** No, this oil won't do, I'm afraid. **c.** No, an irrigation pump won't do, I'm afraid. **d.** No, a mercury switch won't do, I'm afraid. **e.** No, a spanner won't do, I'm afraid. **f.** No, a table won't do, I'm afraid.

4 a. The chief engineer has made up his mind to buy a new computer. **b.** Joan has made up her mind to look for a good secondhand car. **c.** Fred has made up his mind to be a TV technician. **d.** John has made up his mind to serve an apprenticeship. **e.** The policeman has made up his mind to catch the speeder. **f.** Mr Lawrence has made up his mind to sell the company's machines in Germany. **g.** She has made up her mind to buy a transistor radio.

5 b. Mr Smith said he didn't mind talking to the chief engineers first if Mr Miller thought they could help us (*oder:* them). **c.** Mr Smith said he didn't mind buying this generator if Mr Miller thought it was powerful enough. **d.** Mr Smith said he didn't mind repairing the grinding machine first if Mr Miller thought it was necessary. **e.** Mr Smith said he didn't mind designing a new shaft if Mr Miller thought they could do it without a computer. **f.** Mr Smith said that he didn't mind starting again from the beginning if Mr Miller thought there was enough time.

LESSON 16

Zusätzliche Informationen

Briv_high-speed riveting

Die folgenden Ausschnitte aus einem Artikel, der in der Zeitschrift *Engineers' Digest* erschien, zeigen die Hauptvor- und -nachteile herkömmlicher Nietverfahren:

RIVETING has long been (and still is) a reliable technique for the assembly of devices designed to be permanently fastened. The primary advantage of riveting is the low overall cost of the process, i.e., the initial costs of rivets and those of the associated labour and machine time to set the rivets in the parts. Thus, the initial cost of rivets is sub-stantially lower than that of screw-machine parts or special fasteners because rivets are made in large volumes in high-speed heading machines with little scrap loss. Also, assembly costs are generally low, as many types are clinched on high-speed, hopper-fed riveting machines.

Another advantage of the process is its

versatility. For instance, rivets can be used to join dissimilar materials, metallic or non-metallic, in various thicknesses, and can be employed to fasten parts that have already received a final painting or other finishing treatment. At the same time, rivets can be made of any material that can be cold-worked and can have a variety of finishes, such as plating, parkerizing (= *Eisenteile in eine Lösung von Phosphat tauchen, wodurch sich auf der Oberfläche eine feine Schicht Eisenphosphat bildet*), or paint. Moreover, provided that there are flat parallel surfaces for the rivet clinch and head, plus adequate space for the rivet driver during clinching, riveting can be adapted to fasten almost any part shape.

On the other hand, riveting has certain limitations, one of which is that rivets have tensile and fatigue strengths lower than those of comparable bolts or screws, and high tensile loads may pull out the clinch, while severe vibrations may loosen the fastening.

Also, riveted joints are neither watertight nor airtight (although such a joint may be attained at some added cost by using a sealing compound) and cannot, of course, be disassembled for maintenance or replacement without knocking the rivet out and clinching a new rivet in place.

A further limitation of rivets is that they cannot be produced to the same precision as screw-machine parts.

Normal tolerances on the major dimensions of rivets are ±0.005 in., though closer shank-diameter tolerances can be held. Rivets should not be used in applications where dimensional variation must be maintained as low as ±0.001 in.

Any questions?

case-hardening: "the production of a hard surface layer on steel by heating in a carbonaceous medium to increase the carbon content, then quenching"

flame-hardening: "hardening of metal surface by heating with oxyacetylene torch, followed by rapid cooling with water or air jet"

white metal: "usually denotes tin-base alloy (over 50% tin) containing varying amounts of lead, copper, and antimony; used for bearings, domestic articles, and small castings; sometimes also applied to alloys in which lead is the principal metal; also called anti-friction metal, bearing metal"

babbitt metal (*or* **Babbitt's metal**): "a bearing alloy originally patented by Isaac Babbitt, composed of 50 parts tin, 5 antimony, and 1 copper; modern addition of lead greatly extends range of service; composition varies widely, with tin 5% to 90%, copper 1.5% to 6%, antimony 7% to 10%, lead 5% to 48.5%"

Text- und Transferfragen

Briv–high-speed riveting

What is "magazine loading"?

Why do you think magazine loading is more efficient?

What can the Briv system be used for?

Can you explain how it works?

Can you give some examples from industry where rivets are often used?

Why do you think they use rivets?

Any questions?

Can you explain what case-hardening is?

And what is "flame-hardening"?

What are the main components of white metal?

What is white metal used for?

Methodische Hinweise und Schlüssel

1 **a.** But it was checked only yesterday! **b.** But it was filled only a few days ago! **c.** But they were painted only last year! **d.** But they were adjusted only last month! **e.** But it was cleaned only two or three days ago!

2 A1+B4 / A2+B3 / A3+ B5 / A4+B2 / A5+B1 / A6+B6

3 **a.** I wouldn't mind assembling the loudspeaker kit if I had enough time. **b.** I wouldn't mind talking to the managing director if I had enough time. **c.** I wouldn't mind carrying out the experiment if I had enough time. **d.** I wouldn't mind attending the brain-storming session if I had enough time. **e.** I wouldn't mind checking the batteries if I had enough time. **f.** I wouldn't mind visiting the factory if I had enough time. **g.** I wouldn't mind watching TV if I had enough time.

4 **a.** alloy **b.** interior **c.** lead **d.** diameter **e.** approach **f.** surface **g.** antimony

5 Freie Kommunikationsübung, daher kein Schlüssel.

6 Bei den Übersetzungsübungen geht es in der Hauptsache um die Strukturen, weniger um den Wortschatz. Man sollte also den Kursteilnehmern empfehlen, unbekannte oder vergessene Wörter nachzuschlagen. (Wenn noch kein Wörterbuch vorhanden ist, sollten die Kursteilnehmer angehalten werden, jetzt an die Anschaffung zu denken, da gerade bei fortgeschritteneren Lernenden Wörterbücher an Wert gewinnen, weil die verschiedenen angebotenen Übersetzungsmöglichkeiten nun besser relativiert werden können.)
a. You should be extremely careful when installing the aluminium windows. **b.** We weren't able to start work yesterday because we didn't have any rivets. **c.** When the chief engineer arrived he was asked some questions. **d.** The technician said he couldn't help me. **e.** When we arrived the meeting had already started (*oder:* begun). **f.** When is he to fly to Pittsburgh? **g.** Would you mind my calling Mr Lawrence now? (*oder:* Would you mind if I called Mr Lawrence now?) **h.** Have you made up your mind yet? (*oder:* Have you made a

decision yet?) **i.** Unfortunately he didn't know that copper can't be used for such appliances. **j.** I don't mind your smoking *(oder:* I don't mind if you smoke). **k.** He'll have to talk to Mr Miller first.

LESSON 17

Zusätzliche Informationen

The funny side of electronics (II)

Dieser Text wird auf den Tonmaterialien in amerikanischem Englisch erscheinen. Nähere Einzelheiten bezüglich des amerikanischen Englisch finden sich unter „Zusätzliche Informationen", Lektion 4.

color *(US)* = **colour** *(Br.)*

missile: "an object or weapon that is thrown, shot, or otherwise propelled to a target" – "there are two basic types of missile, in the current sense, guided and ballistic; the former is controlled from its launch until it hits its target; the latter, always of long-range, surface-to-surface type, is controlled into a precision ballistic path so that its course cannot be deflected by countermeasures"

Text- und Transferfragen

The funny side of electronics (II)
Where does the story take place?
What is the Senior Officer explaining?
What will happen when the buttons are pressed?
What is the recruit trying to say?

What's new on the market?
What does the new tire do when it is punctured?
What is the inside of the tire made of?
Must the puncturing object be kept in the tread?
What about loss of air?
Can the tire be used in the normal way after the puncturing object has been removed?

Methodische Hinweise und Schlüssel

1 Diese Übung soll zweierlei erreichen: erstens sollen die *question tags* wiederholt werden, zweitens soll ein Kommunikationsanlaß geschaffen werden. Wenn der Teilnehmer also bei b. an einen anderen Teilnehmer die Frage *You can* *tell me where the conversation took place, can't you?* gestellt hat, sollte als Antwort nicht nur *Yes, I can,* sondern auch die Beantwortung der eigentlichen Frage folgen, also z. B. *Yes, I can: It took place in the control room of a missile station.*

2 a. I'll talk to Mr Lawrence, but I'm not sure whether I'll be able to talk to Miss Miller. **b.** I'll buy a battery but I'm not sure whether I'll be able to buy a radial steel tire. **c.** I'll repair the calculator but I'm not sure whether I'll be able to repair the transistor radio. **d.** I'll check the air conditioning unit but I'm not sure whether I'll be able to check the drive motor. **e.** I'll oil the engine but I'm not sure whether I'll be able to oil the milling machine. **f.** I'll paint the walls but I'm not sure whether I'll be able to paint the roof.

3 a. contains **b.** contents **c.** content **d.** contents **e.** contains **f.** content **g.** contain

4 Freie Übung; wegen der Vielzahl der möglichen Antworten kein Schlüssel.

LESSON 18

Zusätzliche Informationen

A jet for $27,500?

Auch hier wieder ein amerikanischer Text (Erläuterungen zum amerikanischen Englisch: unter „Zusätzliche Informationen", Lektion 4).

garage [*Br.:* ˈgærɑːdʒ *oder* ˈgæridʒ *oder* ˈgærɑːʒ; *US:* gəˈrɑːʒ *oder* gəˈrɑːdʒ]

thrust: "propulsive force developed by a jet- or rocket-motor"

Federal Aviation Agency (FAA): "the division of the Department of Commerce that inspects and rates civilian aircraft and airmen and enforces the rules of air safety"

Als Hintergrundinformation noch ein paar Abschnitte aus dem *Newsweek*-Artikel:

Once in the air, there can be other problems. Test pilot Fornof was once on a flight from Atlanta to Washington, D.C., when a defective oil gauge forced him to land on the nearest available strip–which just happened to be Interstate (Highway) 85 near Lexington, N.C. Fornof set the plane down, rolled into a service station and rang the service bell. The attendant's first question: "Is this 'Candid Camera'?" (= *Fernsehserie, in der Menschen heim-*

lich gefilmt wurden, wenn sie auf ungewöhnliche Situationen reagierten; lief in der Bundesrepublik unter dem Titel „Vorsicht, Kamera!") Bede says interest in his planes extends beyond hobbyists: an American firm is trying to sell the jet to the French Air Force as a training plane, and Iran and several South American countries have expressed interest in the BD-5J.

A simple experiment

"When the accumulator is short-circuited by placing a length of thin fuse wire or very thin copper wire across it the wire will immediately melt. Electrical energy is converted into heat energy."

Text- und Transferfragen

A jet for $27,000?
What did a test pilot say about the BD-5J?
How much does the plane cost?
How much is this in German money?
What other technical facts do you remember about the BD-5J?
Is it easy to assemble?
What did one of the customers say about assembling the jet?
What do you think is the Federal Aviation Agency's job? Is such an agency necessary?
What do you think about the idea of offering a plane in kit form?
Do you think you could assemble such a plane if you had the necessary tools?
What other things are offered as kits?

A simple experiment
What happens when you close the switch and send a current through the wire?
Can you explain what sort of conversion has taken place?
Have you ever done such an experiment? (When? Where?)

Methodische Hinweise und Schlüssel

1 Freie Kommunikationsübung, daher kein Schlüssel.

2 a. No, it's a lot narrower than I thought. **b.** No, he's a lot younger than I thought. **c.** No, they're a lot more expensive than I thought. **d.** No, they're a lot nearer than I thought. **e.** No, it's a lot slower than I thought. **f.** No, they're a lot older than I thought.

3 a. by **b.** in **c.** as

4 Diese Übung läßt sich wieder als Hausarbeit einsetzen und müßte dann individuell vom Kursleiter korrigiert werden.

Dabei sollte nicht so sehr auf absolute grammatikalische „Korrektheit" geachtet werden, sondern die erfolgte (oder nicht erfolgte) Kommunikation im Vordergrund stehen.

5 Freie Kommunikationsübung, zu der ebenfalls kein Schlüssel gegeben werden kann. Die Antworten zu a. und b. sind nur Beispiele, die beliebig variiert werden können.

6 Freie Kommunikationsübung, daher kein Schlüssel.

7 a. I don't think so. If he had had the proper tools, he would certainly have checked the computers. **b.** I don't think so. If he had had enough time, he would certainly have flown to London. **c.** I don't think so. If he had known that we need (*oder:* needed) it, he would certainly have sent us the operating manual. **d.** I don't think so. If he had known that there was a policeman, he would certainly have driven more slowly (yesterday).

LESSON 19

Zusätzliche Informationen

Ways of making you drive

dash (*auch:* **dashboard; dash panel; facia; facia panel; instrument panel**) = Instrumententafel

Text- und Transferfragen

Ways of making you drive
What is "ALI"?
Can you explain how it works?
Will it only be used for autobahns?
Will motorists need additional equipment?
What are the advantages of ALI?
Do you think such a system would be useful?

Any questions
Can you explain how a tidal power station works?
Are there any tidal power stations in Germany?
What is the general meaning of "earth" in connection with electricity?
Why do we earth equipment?

Methodische Hinweise und Schlüssel

1 b. He said he was sure that this system would be put into operation. What do you think? **c.** He said he thought that only the German autobahns should be covered. What do you think? **d.** They said driving would be much easier if you had a computer to tell you what to do next. What do you think? **e.** They said the number of accidents would certainly be reduced. What do you think? **f.** They said it would be as easy as using a pocket calculator. What do you think? **g.** They said they wouldn't need any maps in the future. What do you think? **h.** They said every motorist would be happy to spend the forty pounds on his electronic equipment. What do you think? **i.** They said the new system would save a lot of fuel. What do you think? **j.** They said it would be much better than having speed limits on all our roads and autobahns. What do you think?

2 a. oxygen, hydrogen **b.** Oxygen **c.** Sulphur **d.** hydrogen **e.** Sulphur **f.** Oxygen **g.** Carbon **h.** nitrogen **i.** Nitrogen **j.** Carbon **k.** carbon ... carbon

3 Vokabelübung ohne Schlüssel.

4 Diese schriftliche Übung kann wieder als Hausaufgabe eingesetzt werden. Außerdem kann man die fünf zu beantwortenden Punkte zusätzlich noch mündlich abfragen und sie so als mündliche Kommunikationsübung verwenden.

5 a. Well, we might be able to build a bit more later on. **b.** Well, we might need a bit more later on. **c.** Well, you might have to spend a bit more later on. **d.** Well, we might be able to send you a bit more later on.

6 Ohne Schlüssel, da verschiedene Antworten möglich.

7 a. lead **b.** speedometer **c.** alloy **d.** idle **e.** concrete **f.** fuse **g.** plant **h.** furnace **i.** offshore

LESSON 20

Zusätzliche Informationen

A technical drawing

bolt: Schraube mit Mutter *(nut)*, Durchsteckschraube; Bolzen; Riegel

screw: Schraube ohne Mutter, Kopfanziehschraube (ein und dieselbe Schraube muß also je nach Verwendung einmal mit *screw*, das andere mal mit *bolt* übersetzt werden. Schraubensorten, die immer ohne Mutter verwendet werden, können nur mit *screw* übersetzt werden, wie z. B. Holzschrauben).

Anzeige "Technicians"

Nachdem im Handbuch zum *Grundkurs Technik** einige Angaben zu den technischen Ausbildungsgängen in Großbritannien gemacht wurden, soll an dieser Stelle kurz auf die Situation in den USA eingegangen werden (die Erläuterungen stammen aus einem US-Handbuch):

Technicians

Persons can qualify for technician jobs through many combinations of work experience and education because employers traditionally have been flexible in their hiring standards. However, most employers prefer applicants who have had some specialized technical training. Spezialized training is available at technical institutes, junior and community colleges, area vocational-technical schools, extension divisions of colleges and universities, and vocational-technical high schools. Engineering and science students who have not completed the bachelor's degree and others who have degrees in science and mathematics also are able to qualify for technician positions.

Persons can also qualify for technician jobs by less formal methods. Workers may learn through on-the-job training programs or courses in post-secondary or correspondence schools. Some qualify on the basis of experience gained in the Armed Forces. However, post-secondary training is increasingly necessary for advancement to more responsible jobs.

Some of the types of post-secondary and other schools which provide technical training are discussed in the following paragraphs:

Technical Institutes. Technical institutes offer training to qualify students for a job immediately after graduation with a minimum of on-the-job training. In general, students receive intensive technical training but less theory and general education than in engineering schools or liberal arts colleges. A few technical institutes and community colleges offer cooperative programs; students spend part of the time in school and part in paid employment related to their studies. Some technical institutes operate as regular or extension divisions of colleges and universities. Other institutions are operated by States and municipalities, or by private organizations.

Junior and Community Colleges. Curriculums in junior and community colleges which prepare students for technician occupations are similar to those in the freshman and sophomore years of 4-years colleges. After completing the 2-year program, graduates can transfer to 4-year colleges or qualify for some technician jobs. Most large community colleges offer 2-year technical programs, and many employers prefer graduates having more specialized training.

Area Vocational-Technical Schools. These post-secondary public institutions serve students from surrounding areas and train them for jobs in the local area. Most of these schools require a high school degree or its equivalent for admission.

Other Training. Some large corporations conduct training programs and operate private schools to meet their needs for technically trained personnel in specific jobs; such training rarely includes general studies. Training for some technician

---

* Hueber, Ismaning, 1976.

occupations, for instance tool designers and electronic technicians, is available through formal 2- to 4-year apprenticeship programs. The apprentice gets on-the-job training under the close supervision of an experienced technician and related technical knowledge in classes, usually after working hours.

The Armed Forces have trained many technicians, especially in electronics. However, military job requirements are generally different from those in the civilian economy. Thus, military technician training may not be adequate for civilian technician work, and additional training may be necessary for employment.

Technician training also is available from many private technical and correspondence schools that often specialize in a single field such as electronics. Some of these schools are owned and operated by large corporations that have the resources to provide very up-to-date training in a technical field.

Engineers

A bachelor's degree in engineering is the generally accepted educational requirement for beginning engineering jobs. College graduates trained in one of the natural sciences or mathematics also may qualify for some beginning jobs. Experienced technicians with some engineering education are sometimes able to advance to engineering jobs.

Graduate training is being emphasized for an increasing number of jobs; it is essential for most beginning teaching and research positions, and desirable for advancement. Some specialties, such as nuclear engineering, are taught mainly at the graduate level.

About 280 colleges and universities offer a bachelor's degree in engineering. Although programs in the larger branches of engineering are offered in most of these institutions, some small specialties are taught in only a very few. Therefore, students desiring specialized training should investigate curriculums before selecting a college. Admissions requirements for undergraduate engineering schools usually include high school courses in advanced mathematics and the physical sciences.

In a typical 4-year curriculum, the first 2 years are spent studying basic sciences — mathematics, physics, chemistry, introductory engineering — and the humanities, social sciences, and English. The last 2 years are devoted, for the most part, to specialized engineering courses. Some programs offer a general engineering curriculum, permitting the student to choose a specialty in graduate school or acquire it on the job.

Some engineering curriculums require more than 4 years to complete. A number of colleges and universities now offer 5-year master's degree programs. In addition, several engineering schools have formal arrangements with liberal arts colleges whereby a student spends 3 years in liberal arts and 2 years in engineering and receives a bachelor's degree from each.

Some schools have 5- or even 6-year cooperative plans where students coordinate classroom study and practical work experience. In addition to gaining useful experience, students can finance part of their education. Because of the need to keep up with rapid advances in technology, engineers often continue their education throughout their careers in programs sponsored by employers, or in colleges and universities after working hours.

All 50 States and the District of Columbia require licensing for engineers whose work may affect life, health, or property, or who offer their services to the public. In 1974, about 350,000 engineers were registered. Generally, registration requirements include a degree from an accredited engineering school, 4 years of relevant work experience, and the passing of a State examination.

A technical drawing

What does this technical drawing show?

Are the dimensions given in inches?

What about German drawings? Are all dimensions given in millimetres?

"If in doubt, ask? – Do you think this is important? (Why? Why not?)

Do you work with technical drawings in your job? (... in your course? ... in your class?)

Can you make technical drawings?

Have you ever worked with drawings from England or America?

What are technical drawings used for? Who has to work with them?

What's new on the market?

What does this air purifier do?

Where can it be used?

Where is it produced?

What about servicing?

Would it be useful to have such an air purifier in the office or workshop?

Have you ever worked in an air-conditioned room?

Did you like it? What do you think about air conditioning? Does it work properly?

Methodische Hinweise und Schlüssel

1 Schriftliche Übung, auch als Hausaufgabe geeignet; ohne Schlüssel, da freie schriftliche Kommunikation.

2 Die folgende Musterübersetzung dient nur als Beispiel und läßt sich an vielen Stellen variieren:

It was early in the morning.

For some time already, the policeman had been driving behind the car, a brand-new six-cylinder sports car.

The policeman noticed with surprise that the driver of the car was driving extremely slowly and carefully, not more than (*oder:* not faster than) about 25 or 30 miles an hour. And that, although there was no traffic at all. Apart from that, the driver gave all the necessary signals and did not make a single mistake.

The policeman was very much surprised. He had not seen anything like this for a long time. He just had to stop the car and tell the driver that he was driving excellently.

"Don't worry", he said to the sports car driver, "I don't want to give you a ticket. I just want to tell you that you're an excellent driver. If everybody drove as well as you, we wouldn't have any problems and my work would be much easier."

The driver tried to smile. "Yes, you know", he said in an uncertain voice, "when you've drunk as much as I have, you've got to drive carefully, haven't you?"

3 **a.** These milling machines require oiling only twice a week. **b.** These calculators require checking only once a year. **c.** These containers require cleaning only every other week. **d.** These devices require adjusting only once a month. **e.** These tanks require filling only once a week. **f.** These cars require washing only every six weeks. **g.** These hovercraft require servicing only once a week.

TEST B

Dieser Test umfaßt 60 Items. Hinzu kommt ein schriftlicher Testteil ("Writing a letter").

Von den 60 Items sollten etwa 35 richtig gelöst werden, wenn man von einem Bestehen des Testes sprechen will. (Weitere Anmerkungen zu den Tests, besonders hinsichtlich eines zusätzlichen mündlichen Tests, siehe auch unter „TEST A".)

Die Bewertung des Briefes bleibt natürlich ganz dem Kursleiter überlassen. Um eine gewisse Objektivierung zu erreichen, könnte man sich jedoch folgendes Schema vorstellen:

Einleitung und Formalien des Briefes

(Datum, Anrede, Adresse, Abschlußformel usw. . . . . . . 0–4 Punkte

6 Leitpunkte ("Aircraft? Cameras? etc.") . . . . je 3 Punkte
keine oder eine völlig unzureichende Antwort: 0 Punkte
zufriedenstellende Antwort mit Fehlern: 1 Punkt
zufriedenstellende Antwort ohne nennenswerte Fehler: 2 Punkte
gute Antwort ohne oder mit ganz geringfügigen Fehlern:
3 Punkte

Wortschatz und Stil (umfangreicher Wortschatz, passender Stil usw. 0–3 Punkte

Rechtschreibung . . . . 0–2 Punkte

= höchstens 27 Punkte

Es braucht sicherlich nicht betont zu werden, daß das ein relativ grobes Schema ist, das sich im Bedarfsfall noch verfeinern läßt. Für informelle Zwecke (Tests im Rahmen des Unterrichts) ist es aber sicher ausreichend.

Schlüssel und Anmerkungen

(Die folgenden Sätze sollten vom Kursleiter in normaler Sprechgeschwindigkeit vorgelesen werden. Dabei kann man jeden Satz gleich zweimal vorlesen oder aber alle Sätze hintereinander diktieren und dann das Ganze noch einmal vorlesen. Der Lernende schreibt die fehlenden Wörter in die Lücken oder auf ein separates Blatt Papier:)

1 The new engine gives marvellous <u>acceleration</u> right up to a top speed of 160 miles per hour.

2 The two sections of the metal span of the bridge were <u>hoisted</u> 170 feet in the air.

3 Generally speaking, conductivity <u>decreases</u> as the temperature rises.

4 The system involves setting a series of <u>inductive</u> loops into the road surface which pass messages to sensors in cars.

5 The automatic air <u>purifier</u> can be used in every office.

6 The old Jaguar was a very good car but its <u>successor</u> is even better.

7 Our new system reduces <u>wastage</u> to a very low point.

8 Our rivets can be used for a great <u>variety</u> of materials.

9 The tire contains a liner system made of modified <u>sponge</u> rubber with a polyethylene coating.

10 Since the plane is handmade, it will be difficult to get the <u>approval</u> of the Federal Aviation Agency.

11 There is <u>virtually</u> no loss of air when a nail penetrates the tire.

12 The rivet is finally installed and the mandrel <u>withdrawn</u>.

13 Suddenly, the <u>buckled</u> section of the bridge changed colour.

(Wie bei allen anderen Übersetzungsübungen, so sind auch bei diesem Test die angegebenen Lösungsvorschläge nur als Beispiele anzusehen:)

(14) For a long time now, riveting has been among the most reliable fastening techniques. **(15)** It is used when different components (*oder:* parts) are to be permanently fastened. **(16)** One of the main advantages of this fastening technique is the low overall cost, particularly the low cost of the rivets. **(17)** This comes from the fact that rivets are produced (*oder:* manufactured) in large volumes (*oder:* in large quantities). **(18)** Apart from that, assembly costs are generally low, too, since many types of rivets can be used in high-speed riveting machines. **(19)** Of course, rivets have their disadvantages, too: The tensile strength, for example, is usually lower than that of screws or bolts. **(20)** Besides (*oder:* In addition), strong vibration may loosen the rivets. **(21)** In the last few years, however, new riveting methods have been developed which offer greater tensile strength.

22a 23a 24b 25c 26a 27b 28a 29d 30d 31b 32a 33c 34d 35d 36c 37c 38c 39a 40d 41c 42c 43d 44c

45 with ... off in **46** of **47** in ... about ... of **48** in ... of ... for **49** on **50** to ... by ... of **51** of ... on ... up **52** to ... in ... in **53** to ... at

54 in about **55** for ... for ... to **56** For ... to **57** on **58** in **59** up ... to ... to **60** on

Writing a letter

Siehe Vorbemerkungen zu „TEST B".

Zusätzliche Informationen

Fiesta – Ford's Euro car

bhp (= horsepower): "true horsepower absorbed by a horsepower meter which is called a 'brake' or a dynamometer, as distinct from fiscal or taxation horsepower (e.g. 2CV in France) which is related to engine capacity or the stroke and bore dimensions by some arbitrary formula; always look for net or DIN figures which give the power output of an engine as installed in the car; SAE figures *(SAE = Society of Automotive Engineers)* often represent gross output with special exhaust system and auxiliaries such as generator and cooling fan removed" *(Die nach der SAE in den USA gemessene Leistung ist um ca. 15 bis 20 Prozent größer als nach DIN-Vorschrift.)* – 1 PS = 0,7355 kW, 1 kW = 1,36 PS

gearbox: "a transmission, as in an automobile *(US)*"

McPherson-Achse: „... ist eine neuerdings auch bei frontgetriebenen Personenwagen häufig verwendete Vorderachskonstruktion, die nur geringe Änderungen von Sturz *(= camber),* Spreizung *(= kingpin inclination)* und Spurweite *(= track width)* beim Einfedern aufweist. Die platzsparende Bauweise des McPherson-Federbeins wird durch die Kombination von Feder und Stoßdämpfer *(= shock absorber)* sowie durch die Funktion des Dämpferrohrs als Achsschenkel erzielt. Beim Lenken dreht sich die komplette Einheit, die am unteren Ende den Achszapfen mit der Radlagerung und den Lenkhebel trägt, um einen Kugelbolzen und die Stoßdämpfer-Kolbenstange, deren oberes Ende an der Karosserie befestigt ist. McPherson-Achsen ermöglichen große Federwege und weiches Ansprechen der Federung, sie reagieren jedoch empfindlich auf Unwucht an den Rädern."

pushrod "a rod through which the tappet *(= Stößel)* of an overhead valve engine operates the rocker arm *(= Kipphebel),* when the crankshaft is located in the crankcase"

Text- und Transferfragen	**Fiesta – Ford's Euro car** Where is the Fiesta built? Can you tell me who its competitors on the German market are? *(Wenn nötig,* competitor *erklären!)* What do you know about its engine? What did they say in the test report? Which do you like better: manual gearboxes or automatic ones? What are the advantages of manual gearboxes?

Have you ever driven a car with an automatic gearbox?

What do you think about cars in the same class as the Fiesta? *(z. B. Polo, Golf, Fiat, Mini usw.)*

Which of them do you think is the best?

What do you think about cars from England? Are they as good as German cars, or are they better? What about French, Italian, Japanese cars?

Have you ever driven an American car? What do you think about American cars?

Any questions?

Do you remember what the word "laser" means?

What are lasers used for? *(z. B. für chirurgische Zwecke, besonders bei Augenoperationen; zum Bohren feiner Löcher und für andere industrielle Zwecke)*

Have you ever seen a radar unit in operation? (Where?)

What does the word "radar" mean?

What are radar units used for? Where are they used?

Methodische Hinweise und Schlüssel

1. b. John suggested that we should have the whole thing designed by a computer. **c.** John suggested (that it would be much better) to have it repaired by an expert. **d.** John suggested that we could (*oder:* should) get the new model tested on the road. **e.** John suggested that we should think of getting it designed from scratch (*oder:* ... should get it designed ...).

2 a. Well, he told me he had already got them licensed in Germany. **b.** Well, he told me he had already got it painted in Germany. **c.** Well, he told me he had already got them serviced in Germany. **d.** Well, he told me he had already got it repaired in Germany.

3 a. Why don't you have (*oder:* get) transistors installed? **b.** We should have told him that he must have (*oder:* get) the drilling machine oiled. **c.** Did you have (*oder:* get) the letter translated yesterday? **d.** When will you have (*oder:* get) the oil level checked? **e.** Why don't you have (*oder:* get) it explained by the chief engineer? **f.** We want to have (*oder:* get) new solar panels built in (*oder:* installed) next year. **g.** Have (*oder:* get) the appliances checked before you start work(ing). **h.** We will have to have (*oder:* get) the engines cleaned.

4 Freie Kommunikationsübung, daher kein Schlüssel.

5 a. On ... on **b.** to ... at **c.** to ... of **d.** for **e.** at ... near

Zusätzliche Informationen

Solar heating

Als Hintergrundinformation einige Passagen aus der Zeitschrift *Do it yourself*, die sich mit Sonnenkollektoren befassen:

The majority of proprietary collectors fall into two main categories:

Metal absorber solar collectors

These are usually housed in a shallow case which is often glazed at the front. Usually a strip of aluminium foil is placed immediately behind the absorber plate and then a layer of insulation to prevent heat loss from the back of the case. The absorber plate, which invariably has matt black finish, may have water pipes bonded to its surface or integral waterways, such as in a steel central heating radiator.

Plastic matrix absorber collectors

These are a fairly recent development. Black plastic is extruded so that waterways are incorporated within the thickness of a two-skin layer. This allows the water to spread over the back of virtually the entire collector layer. The matrix can be used in an insulated casing, but it is usually placed in a simple frame or rack and used unglazed. As yet the life span of this type of panel is unknown, although it is claimed they are impervious to pool chemicals and should be good for at least ten years. Indeed one manufacturer guarantees his panel for this period.

What's new on the market?

Der vollständige Text der Anzeige bietet noch einige nützliche Informationen:

These Tuf-lok nuts have the nylon patch applied to the threads by spraying. Both ends of the thread are clear of nylon to allow easy alignment and start of the bolt. With this locking feature the nuts are claimed to be vibration-proof to values in excess of BS (= *British Standard*) 3692, BS 1768 and BS 1083. The locking medium is impervious to petrol most chemicals and temperatures in the range —56°C to 120°C.

The ability of these nuts to be used in either direction is particularly suited to automatic nut runner operation and fast assembly line production. It is said that compared with conventional nylon ring-type self-locking nuts, the Tuf-lok can represent a cost saving of between 20 and 40 per cent.

Text- und Transferfragen

Solar heating

What are the solar panels in this text used for? (= *They heat a domestic hot water tank.*)

Can you explain the basic principles of the system?

What is the panel system filled with in winter?

What do you think about solar energy? Will it help to solve our energy problems?

What other sources of energy do you know? (= *oil, water, gas, coal, wind, waves, etc.*) What are the main advantages or disadvantages of these energy sources?

What's new on the market?
What is unusual about the new nuts?
Where are they produced?
Why are both ends of the thread clear of nylon?
What other things is nylon used for?

Methodische Hinweise und Schlüssel

1 a. Well, they probably haven't got anyone who knows anything about translating leaflets. **b.** Well, they probably haven't got anyone who knows anything about checking temperature switches. **c.** Well, they probably haven't got anyone who knows anything about repairing pumps. **d.** Well, they probably haven't got anyone who knows anything about programming computers. **e.** Well, they probably haven't got anyone who knows anything about installing aluminium windows.

2 a. technical draughtsman **b.** car mechanic **c.** pilot **d.** policeman

3 a. I'd rather go to the USA, if you don't mind. **b.** I'd rather fly, if you don't mind. **c.** I'd rather go to New York, if you don't mind. **d.** I'd rather work in an office, if you don't mind. **e.** I'd rather live in an apartment, if you don't mind. **f.** I'd rather have an American car, if you don't mind. **g.** I'd rather work during the day, if you don't mind. **h.** I'd rather go this year, if you don't mind.

4 Wie schon die vorherigen schriftlichen Übungen dieser Art, so eignet sich auch diese als Hausaufgabe, da sie in den meisten Fällen im Unterricht zu viel Zeit wegnehmen würde. Kein Schlüssel, da freie Kommunikationsübung.

5 GERMAN VISITOR: Excuse me, sir, could you tell me where I can find the nearest garage?
ENGLISHMAN: Yes, certainly. Second street to the right.
GERMAN VISITOR: Thank you very much, sir.
ENGLISHMAN: You're welcome (*oder:* Not at all.).

GERMAN VISITOR: Could I have a leaflet about the machine, please?
ENGINEER: Yes ... here you are.
GERMAN VISITOR: Thank you.
ENGINEER: Not at all (*oder:* You're welcome.).

GERMAN VISITOR: <u>Oh, I'm sorry.</u> I didn't know you were reading the newspaper.
HOTEL GUEST: That's all right. Never mind.

GERMAN VISITOR: <u>Pardon?</u>
ENGLISHMAN: I said how long have you been here now?
GERMAN VISITOR: About a week, I think.

CHIEF ENGINEER: Mr Miller, may I introduce you to Mr Baldinger, our German representative . . .
MR BALDINGER: <u>How do you do.</u>
MR MILLER: How do you do.

LESSON 23

Zusätzliche Informationen

Space age shooting gallery (amerikanische Sprecher auf den Tonträgern)

fresnel lens: "one built up of a number of narrow concentric segments, used where a flat surface is desirable as in the field lens of viewfinders *(= Sucher)* or the viewing screen of reflex cameras"

psi: pounds per square inch *(= Pfund pro Quadratinch);* 1 psi = 703,066 Kilogramm je Quadratmeter

.357 Magnum: Revolverkaliber, etwa 11,5 mm.

Any questions?

electromagnet: "soft iron core, embraced by a current-carrying coil, which exhibits appreciable magnetic effects only when current passes"

transistor: "three-electrode semi-conductor *(= Halbleiter)* device"

Text- und
Transferfragen

Space age shooting gallery
What does the new revolver use instead of bullets?
What does the revolver look like? *(= It looks like a normal revolver.)*
What do you know about the target?
How does the system work?
What can it be used for?

Any questions?

What is an electromagnet?

What is a coil?

Can you tell me what transistors are?

What are they used for?

Are transistors easily damaged?

Why are transistors better than valves?

Methodische Hinweise und Schlüssel

1 Freie Kommunikationsübung, daher ohne Schlüssel.

2 Diese Übung eignet sich wieder als Hausaufgabe. Sollte es erforderlich sein, kann man ganz kurz erklären, was in einer Zusammenfassung dieser Art enthalten sein muß: *Um was geht es? Was ist neu? Wie funktioniert es? Wer könnte sich dafür interessieren?* usw. An eine Einführung in die sehr spezielle Form des *Précis* ist allerdings an dieser Stelle nicht gedacht.

3 a. – **b.** The . . . – . . . – . . . –

4 Freie Kommunikationsübung, daher ohne Schlüssel.

5 a. Well, I think you'd better tell the chief engineer that you don't want to work there. **b.** Well, I think you'd better tell the chief engineer that you don't want to talk to them. **c.** Well, I think you'd better tell the chief engineer that you don't want to use it. **d.** Well, I think you'd better tell the chief engineer that you don't want to translate it. **e.** Well, I think you'd better tell the chief engineer that you don't want to write it. **f.** Well, I think you'd better tell the chief engineer that you don't want to work there.

6 a. Have you already read the article about the new laser activated shooting gallery? **b.** Yes, I found it very interesting. **c.** Do you think we'll soon have such shooting galleries in Germany, too? **d.** I don't know . . . perhaps in a few years. It would be interesting, anyway.

LESSON 24

Zusätzliche Informationen

Pneumatically or electrically operated tools?

Die folgenden Abschnitte des Originalartikels zeigen weitere Zusammenhänge auf:

It is generally conceded that, in certain special applications where safety is of prime importance, e.g., in hazardous atmospheres, pneumatically powered tools are preferable to electrically powered types because they eliminate the risk of fire or explosion from possible sparking or arcing of electrical components. In most other applications, however, the question of whether to use pneumatic or electric portable tools has sometimes been the subject of heated discussion. Nowadays, there seems less point in being dogmatic about the type of power used and, in fact, there is no clear-cut answer to the question, as the choice of drive is determined by a number of criteria, chief among which are the following:—

(1) The source of energy already available on site.
(2) The type of operation (continuous or intermittent) and the resulting power consumption.
(3) The size and power/weight ratio of the tool (also to be considered in the light of operating time).
(4) The comparative ease of servicing and maintenance.

These criteria and others, insofar as they apply to different types of portable pneumatic and electric tools, are discussed below.

Drilling and Tapping Tools

Both pneumatically and electrically powered drills are widely used in industry today, and it is extremely difficult to assess their comparative advantages and disadvantages, as they can be decided only in relation to each particular application. It is generally true, however, that pneumatic drills with capacities up to about 12 mm in diameter are smaller in size and weight than equivalent electric drills operating on normal or high frequencies. On the other hand, steplessly variable speed, which has long been cited as an argument in favour of pneumatically powered drills, no longer seems valid, as a large number of electric drills are now available with electronically controlled infinitely variable speed facilities.

In particular, electric drills have undergone many stages of development. For instance, in the early days of portable electric tools, a 4-mm drill weighed 7.5 kg, whereas the equivalent tool now weighs only about 1.2 kg. Even so, a pneumatic drill of the same capacity is still very much lighter, i.e., about 0.5 kg. Similar considerations apply to tapping tools, the pneumatic versions normally being appreciably lighter, as the vane-type air motor generally used is reversible and therefore does not require a reverse gear.

Screwdrivers and Nutrunners

As already indicated, portable powered screwdrivers and nutrunners play an appreciable part in the mechanization of assembly operations. The pneumatic versions appear to have an advantage over their electric counterparts, notably in regard to their much higher power/weight ratio.

In general, it should be noted that the range of types available is much greater in the case of pneumatic screwdrivers and nutrunners. The reason is their typical unit construction system, which enables the user to specify a tool with the optimum power, speed, and equipment for each operation. The housing can be a pistol-grip or a straight design, while the clutch can be a simple direct-drive or dog, an adjustable slipping or torque- limiting type, or an automatic design. In addition, the head of the tools can cater for nutrunning or for screwdriving, using bits with or without a locating sleeve, and special versions can be provided with angle heads for nutrunning or screwdriving, again using bits with or without a locating sleeve.

Some of these tools are equipped with pneumatically controlled torque-limiting devices, tools of this nature being widely used in the automotive industry, which appears to have a fundamental preference for pneumatic screwdrivers and nutrunners. It may also be mentioned that some firms even issue certificates ("preferred", "acceptable", or "conditional") for various makes of screwdrivers and nutrunners after prolonged tests. Before being classified as "preferred" such a pneumatic tool must endure at least 500,000 load cycles, during which the torque must be held within narrow tolerances.

A simple experiment

accumulator: "Voltaic cell which can be charged and discharged; on charge, when an electric current is passed through it into the positive and out of the negative terminals (according to the conventional direction of flow of current), electrical energy is converted into chemical energy; the process is reversed on discharge, the chemical energy, less losses both in potential and current, being converted into useful electrical energy; accumulators therefore form a useful portable supply of electric power, but have the disadvantages of being heavy and of being at best 70% efficient; more often known as battery, also called reversible cell, secondary cell, storage battery"

Erläuterungen zum Experiment: "... The cotton round the thinner wire will soon start to burn, and the wire becomes red hot and may even melt. A pupil should be asked to feel the thicker wire. He should find that it is quite cool. The pupils should be asked to think out why it is the thinner wire that heats up. The answer is that it requires more energy for the electrons to overcome the resistance of the thinner wire, and this is the energy which is converted into heat."

Text- und Transferfragen

Pneumatically or electrically powered tools?
Can you tell me when pneumatic tools are preferable? (Why?)
Is it possible to say which of the two – pneumatically or electrically powered tools – have a better efficiency?
What about maintenance?

A simple experiment
What is an accumulator?
What are accumulators used for?
What other things do you need for this experiment?
Can you explain what happens when the current is switched on?

Methodische Hinweise und Schlüssel

1 Freie Kommunikationsübung, daher ohne Schlüssel.

2 Wie Übung 1.

3 a. anti-corrosion **b.** nonconductor **c.** inaccurate **d.** improper **e.** Antifreeze **f.** improbable **g.** non-magnetic

4 a. As far as this machine is concerned, steel seems to be the best material. **b.** As far as batteries are concerned, mercury seems to be the best material. **c.** As far as these boxes are concerned, plastic seems to be the best material. **d.** As far as the conductors are concerned, copper seems to be the best material. **e.** As far as this building project is concerned, concrete seems to be the best material. **f.** As far as this roof is concerned, glass seems to be the best material. **g.** As far as these conveyors are concerned, cold-rolled steel seems to be the best material.

5 Freie Kommunikationsübung, daher ohne Schlüssel.

6 a. didn't he? **b.** don't they? **c.** will she? **d.** don't they? **e.** can't you? **f.** isn't it? **g.** would he? **h.** don't you? **i.** don't you? **j.** did he? **k.** was he?

LESSON 25

Zusätzliche Informationen

baseboard *(US):* "board forming the foot of an interior wall"; *(Br.:)* skirting board

transformer: "an electrical device without any moving parts, which transfers energy of an alternating current in the primary winding to that in one or more secondary windings, through electromagnetic induction"

Text- und Transferfragen
What does the company in this advertisement offer?
How is the Shock-M-All system installed?
Where can it be used?
What does a transformer do?
Why is a transformer needed for this system?
What happens when a cockroach crawls through the opening?
Is the system dangerous for small children?
What about maintenance?

How much does the system cost?
How much is that in German money?
Do you think it is expensive?
What do you think about the idea?

Methodische Hinweise und Schlüssel

1 **a.** that **b.** Which **c.** that **d.** which (*oder:* that) **e.** which

2 **a.** Well, then we'd better send them a technician who really knows something about batteries. **b.** Well, then we'd better send them a technician who really knows something about baseboards. **c.** Well, then we'd better send them a technician who really knows something about transformers. **d.** Well, then we'd better send them a technician who really knows something about pneumatically powered tools.

3 **a.** rivet **b.** valve **c.** piston **d.** switch **e.** lathe

4 **a.** He told me he wanted to get them installed by a technician. **b.** He told me he wanted to get it repaired by a technician. **c.** He told me he wanted to get it assembled by a technician.

5 **a.** misreading **b.** pre-stressed **c.** unemployed **d.** disapproves **e.** dissatisfied **f.** multi-spindle **g.** disagreeable

6 Freie Kommunikationsübung, daher ohne Schlüssel.

7 **a.** to **b.** out . . . on **c.** about (*oder:* approximately) **d.** in . . . in . . . of . . . in **e.** in . . . in **f.** about (*oder:* of) **g.** to . . . under

LESSON 26

Zusätzliche Informationen

CAD – computer-aided design (I)

Als Hintergrundinformation noch einige Abschnitte aus einem Artikel über CAD in der englischen Zeitschrift *Engineering*:

The preparation of data for computer programs is often tedious. The description of a component can be given in words, but a picture or sketch would be much easier and more relevant. The latter task can be undertaken by a computer, although the emphasis is now being placed on the use of graphics to verify the data input and show up faults on the screen.

The computer can and is being used to produce drawings. Software is available and this can be manipulated by the user to generate the basic elements of the drawing. Basically, a line is defined by its end points and a program can then be used to produce a large sequence of end points from which complicated objects can easily be drawn. These lines can be drawn in three dimensions. It is possible to take groups of lines, store them away for future use and, thus, build up a library of parts.

For example, it is possible to define a bolt once only and, subsequently, to make use of this description in different parts of the drawing. Since the computer can make rapid calculations and, in general, bolts are of the same shape though the dimensions may vary, it is possible, having defined the general shape, to use this shape with varying parameters so that it becomes correctly scaled and the relevant lengths are adjusted to meet the user's requirements.

Similarly, a computer can generate a series of common shapes such as boxes, cones, spheres, cylinders, etc and build them into accepted engineering objects. By using these techniques and so having the ability to effectively draw lines free hand, it is possible to build up engineering drawings by means of an interactive terminal. The drawings can then be output on to a plotter (= *automatic drafting machine*).

What's new on the market?

Die Illustration im Lehrbuch wird in der betreffenden Westinghouse-Broschüre folgendermaßen beschrieben:

An X-ray image of the tread of the tire seen through the window of this lead-lined room is shown displayed on the television monitor in the foreground. The image shows a break in the cord layer of the tire. To the right of the television monitor is the control console of the tire testing system.

One of six different types of systems developed thus far by the Westinghouse Astronuclear Laboratory, this equipment is designated the STX-400 tire inspection system. It is intended for production line sampling of all sizes of passenger car tires and small sizes of truck and bus tires.

For complete inspection, the tire is rotated in three different positions at rates up to three inches per second to expose all of the tread, sidewalls and bead regions. The pedestal on which the tire is mounted turns in a horizontal plane to present either the sidewalls or the tread to the camera.

Text- und Transferfragen

CAD – computer-aided design (I)
Can you explain what "CAD" is?
What is CAD used for?
How can CAD be used in the motor industry?
How can CAD help in the construction of the body of a car?
What is "punched tape"?
What is a "graphics display"?

What's new on the market?
What does Westinghouse use to inspect tires?
What does X-ray inspection show?

How does the system operate?

What other things are X-rays used for in industry?

(Inspection of weldings, for instance.)

Why does the operator stay in a lead-lined room when the X-ray equipment is used?

What does the operator use to check the process? *(Screen!)*

Methodische Hinweise und Schlüssel

1 TELEPHONIST: Leicester Engineering Company. Good morning.

MR BALDINGER: Good morning. This is Mr Baldinger. Is Mr Lawrence there, please? Extension 367, I think.

TELEPHONIST: Mr Baldinger? Oh yes, of course. You're calling from Germany, aren't you?

MR BALDINGER: Yes, I am.

TELEPHONIST: Hold on a moment, I'll put you through to Mr Lawrence ... No ... the line's busy, I'm afraid. He's engaged just now.

MR BALDINGER: Could you ask him to call me back? I'll be in the office all morning, I think.

TELEPHONIST: Wait a minute ... I'll try again ... Yes, I've got him on the line now ...

MR LAWRENCE: Lawrence speaking.

MR BALDINGER: Hallo, Mr Lawrence. This is Walter Baldinger.

MR LAWRENCE: Oh, hello, Mr Baldinger. What can I do for you?

MR BALDINGER: I'm calling about the conveyors you said were dispatched some time ago. They haven't arrived yet.

MR LAWRENCE: Well, that's most unfortunate. I'm going to take care of that immediately. By the way, the leaflets in German have arrived by now, haven't they?

MR BALDINGER: Yes, they have. They're very useful, I must say.

MR LAWRENCE: Fine. And don't worry about the delay. I'll see to it that you get everything on time in the future.

MR BALDINGER: Yes, that would help me a lot.

MR LAWRENCE: Well, thanks for calling me, Mr. Baldinger. Hope to see you next month in London at the fair.

MR BALDINGER: Yes, I hope so, too. Good-bye, then.

MR LAWRENCE: Good-bye, Mr. Baldinger.

2 Freie Kommunikationsübung, daher kein Schlüssel.

3 Wie Übung 2.

LESSON 27

Zusätzliche Informationen

CAD – computer-aided design (II)

$2 \cdot 5 \times 10^{-6}$ two point five times ten to the power of minus six

Sollte der Unterrichtsverlauf es erforderlich machen, kann man auf einige der folgenden mathematischen Zeichen und Formeln und ihre Aussprache eingehen:

$\sqrt{a + b}$ square root of (the sum of) a plus b

[a+b] a plus b in brackets *oder* bracket open a plus b bracket close

(a+b) a plus b in parantheses

$X^{-1} \cdot X^3$ X to the power (of) minus one times X cubed

$X^{-2} \cdot X^4$ X to the power (of) minus two times X to the power (of) four

$h = \dfrac{v \cdot t}{2} = \dfrac{g \cdot t^2}{2}$ h equals v times t, all over two, equals g times t squared, all over two

$\left(\dfrac{a}{b}c + d \right)$ a over b times c, plus d, all in parantheses

A simple experiment

Erläuterungen zum Experiment: "The compass needle is placed near the end of the coil so that when the current is switched on the needle deflects. The conversion is

electrical energy → magnetic energy → kinetic energy.

Other practical examples of this conversion: telephone, electric bell, gramophone pick-up."

Text- und Transferfragen

CAD – computer-aided design (II)

How can CAD be used in connection with car tests?
Why are normal car tests expensive?
How is the crash victim represented in the CAD test?
Have you ever seen a crash test? (Where? Can you tell us something about it?)
What do you think about crash tests?

A simple experiment
What do you need for this experiment?
What happens to the compass needle when the current is
switched on?
Can you explain what energy conversions have taken
place?

Methodische Hinweise und Schlüssel

1 a. All the nuts in this box will be used for assembling the machine tools.
b. All the data in this computer will be used for designing the bridge. **c.** All
the steel sections in this plant will be used for building the conveyors. **d.** All
the drawings on this table will be used for constructing the new car. **e.** All the
nuclear power stations in this country will be used for producing energy. **f.** All
the solar panels in this workshop will be used for heating Mr Sharpley's house.
g. All the computers in this room will be used for orbiting the rockets. **h.** All
the operating manuals on this workbench will be used for training our service
technicians. **i.** All the instruments on this table will be used for checking the
furnaces.

2 a. stormy **b.** generalize **c.** wasteful **d.** welder **e.** measurable **f.** doubtless
g. untranslatable **h.** absorber **i.** magnetize **j.** dirty **k.** limitless **l.** acceptable
m. burner **n.** specialize **o.** recorder

3 Freie Kommunikationsübung, daher ohne Schlüssel.

4 a. After studying the drawings, they started programming the computer.
b. After reading the letter, they started translating it. **c.** After charging the
battery, they started repairing the brakes. **d.** After checking the temperature
switch, they started filling the cold water tank.

5 b. I'm sure he would have carried out the experiment if the chief engineer
hadn't told him to program(me) the computer first. **c.** I'm sure he would have
calculated the victim trajectory if the chief engineer hadn't told him to calcu-
late other criteria first. **d.** I'm sure he would have assembled the loudspeakers
if the chief engineer hadn't told him to install the tuners first. **e.** I'm sure he
would have gone to London if the chief engineer hadn't told him to go to
Birmingham first.

LESSON 28

Zusätzliche Informationen

Der Text stammt aus einer amerikanischen Broschüre und wird auf den Tonmaterialien in amerikanischem Englisch gesprochen.

orbit: "the path of a heavenly body (and, by extension, an artificial satellite, spacecraft, etc.) moving about another under gravitational attraction"

torus: = Torus *oder* Kreisring *oder* Wulst

hub: "the centre part of a wheel"

light industry: = Leichtindustrie *oder* Konsumgüterindustrie

silicon: "non-metallic element, symbol Si; silicates are the chief constituents of many rocks, clays, and soils; silicon is manufactured by reducing silica with carbon in an electric furnace, and is used in glass and in making certain alloys; it has semi-conducting properties, being used for transistors and certain crystal diodes"

rocket booster *oder* **booster rocket:** "a rocket, usually jettisonable, used to assist the acceleration of missiles"

Text- und Transferfragen	
Text- und	What did the study group recommend?
Transferfragen	What did they say about the engineering problems?
	What would the space colony look like?
	What would be done to simulate normal earth weight?
	What could the inhabitants of such a space colony do? (What jobs could they have?)
	Where would they get their food from?
	What do you think about the idea? Would you like to live in such a space colony for some time? Do you think we need such colonies in the future? (Why? Why not?)

Methodische Hinweise und Schlüssel

1 Um Zeit zu sparen, empfiehlt es sich, das Lesen der Anzeige als Hausaufgabe zu stellen. Im Unterricht kann man sich dann ganz auf die mündliche Seite konzentrieren und dabei den Kursteilnehmern die angegebenen Fragen stellen. Danach – vielleicht in der folgenden Unterrichtsstunde – kann man die gleichen Fragen noch einmal von Teilnehmer 1 zu Teilnehmer 2 usw. stellen lassen.

2 Auch diese Übung eignet sich als Hausaufgabe und müßte dann vom Kursleiter individuell nachgesehen werden. Sowohl Übung 1 als auch Übung 2 sind freie Kommunikationsübungen und daher ohne Schlüssel.

3 a. And what sort of metal were they made of? **b.** And what did he talk about? **c.** And what did he want to complain about? **d.** And what was she thinking about? **e.** And who was it programmed by? **f.** And which leaflets was he interested in?

4 Freie Kommunikationsübung, daher ohne Schlüssel.

LESSON 29

Zusätzliche Informationen

Diese Lektion ist die letzte, die auf den Tonmaterialien in amerikanischem Englisch gesprochen wird.

hypersonic: "noting or pertaining to speed that is at least five times that of sound in the same medium"

Mach number: "the ratio of the speed of a body, or of the flow of a fluid, to the speed of sound in the same medium; at Mach 1, speed is sonic (= Schallgeschwindigkeit); below Mach 1, it is subsonic; above Mach 1, it is supersonic, creating a Mach (or shock) wave"

Text- und Transferfragen

What do you think?
– Does NASA do more than fly to the moon?
– Are there enough space benefits? Can you think of any?
– Do the Americans spend too much money on space research?
– Are speeds in excess of four or five Mach really necessary?
– Will we have planes with speeds like that in the near future?
– Should Germany spend more money on space research?
– What are communications satellites used for?
– Should we build our own German communications satellites? (Why? Why not?)

Methodische Hinweise und Schlüssel

1 **a.** right **b.** wrong **c.** wrong **d.** right **e.** wrong **f.** right **g.** right

2 **b.** Well, I wonder if he'd been able to charge it even if it hadn't been too old. **c.** Well, I wonder if he'd been able to carry it out even if he'd known how to use an accumulator. **d.** Well, I wonder if he'd been able to fly it even if he'd had a second pilot.

3 Freie Kommunikationsübung, daher ohne Schlüssel.

4 **a.** Temperatures in excess of $40°$ C mustn't be used. **b.** Speeds in excess of 100 mph mustn't be used. **c.** Cylinder diameters in excess of 5 in mustn't be used. **d.** Engines in excess of 500 pounds mustn't be used.

5 **a.** give **b.** take **c.** Take **d.** Give **e.** take

6 Schriftliche Kommunikationsübung, die sich wieder als Hausaufgabe eignet. Zur Kontrolle des Gelernten und zur Korrektur der Fehler sollten die Briefe dann vom Kursleiter individuell nachgesehen werden.

7 Freie Kommunikationsübung, daher ohne Schlüssel.

LESSON 30

Zusätzliche Informationen

The end of the assembly line?

Als weitere Diskussionsgrundlagen folgen zwei Ausschnitte aus englischen Publikationen. Der erste betrifft die neuen Arbeitsmethoden in Schweden und stammt aus der Zeitschrift *Autocar*; der zweite befaßt sich mit Schichtarbeit und wurde der *Sunday Times* entnommen:

... Another important problem posed by the TUC (= *Trades Union Congress: official representative body of British trade unions*) is whether at a time when workers want more leisure, more flexibility and choice in their lives, and control over their own activities, it is desirable to encourage economic pressures for patterns of working hours which will, in general, tend to act in the opposite direction.

The TUC is against leaving the individual worker free to make a judgment between an increase in his income for shift working and the sacrifice of leisure. It argues that the worker most likely to accept shift working and the higher earnings that it brings is the man with heavy family and financial commitments who is young enough and healthy enough to be willing to stand the disturbance that accompanies shift work ...

The TUC estimates that more than one-third of Britain's 24 million work force is now involved in shift working against 22% four years ago...

As shift work is extended so the demands for special social facilities will also grow like the provision of medical, canteen and transport facilities.

Although the TUC admits that the evidence is conflicting and inconclusive the document says that "there seems little doubt that shift working has some adverse effect on health particularly in the case of night working."

The TUC adds: "Where shifts are rapidly rotated, though this reduces the length of time on unpopular afternoon and night shifts there is evidence of disturbance to health.

"Despite this evidence it must be accepted that some workers seem able to adapt themselves to shift working without suffering adverse effects on health and apparently without significantly increasing their chances of dying."

"What remains doubtful is whether given the enormous expansion in shift working the general health of a significant proportion of industrial manual workers is not being affected to some degree."

The TUC is also maintaining its ban on night work by women in factories until equal pay is generally applicable and it sees no strong social reasons for not continuing the restrictions on shift working by young workers.

Ironically the document ends by noting that in Sweden and Norway night work is prohibited for both men and women...

As British Leyland management and unions continue their apparently endless wrangling over the introduction of Measured Day Working and piece work rates before going over to the new system, we wonder if both sides are taking careful note of the goings-on in the motor industry across the North Sea, in Sweden. There managements have realized that with an intensive secondary and further education programme it is becoming increasingly difficult to recruit and retain workers to man boring, tedious and monotonous assembly work.

Volvo have been looking at a new system of vehicle production which in effect tends to eliminate the assembly line, and sets gangs of workers to building complete individual cars. Although much more expensive than the assembly line, this method, it is claimed, cuts down absenteeism, increases interest and promotes competition between groups. Workers choose which tasks they will perform, pick a leader, set their own tea and lunch breaks, and even in some cases fix their working day.

Now Saab Scania have announced a new engine assembly system for their two-litre Saab 99 engine at Sodertajle based on the same premise.

The assembly line goes, and "autonomous assembly groups" take over final assembly of the units.

So far, say Saab, the experiment has not been going long enough to permit far reaching conclusions, but generally monotony is reduced, and motivation and job satisfaction are increased.

Much of the new engine plant is automated and as heavy work is done automatically, a high proportion of women have also been employed in the gangs.

Considering the battles British Leyland and many other of the car giants have had in the past to get through new production and assembly techniques, we see little hope of this sort of idea being adopted in the near future here. But that is a great pity, because for once both management and workers could benefit enormously. Could it be that both sides are now too deeply entrenched in their respective camps ever again to cross no man's land and talk about the future of the industry?

Entsprechend der vorhandenen Zeit kann man dieses zusätzliche Material mehr oder weniger stark gekürzt in den Unterricht einfließen lassen. In jedem Fall sollten aber dem Teilnehmer die wesentlichen Aussagen bekannt gemacht werden, da sich einige der Fragen unter „Text- und Transferfragen" darauf beziehen.

What's new on the market?

Die folgende Beschreibung der Funktion dient als Hintergrundinformation und muß nicht unbedingt in den Unterricht einfließen:

A crystal-controlled reference is used to drive a chain of 15 binary dividers which reduce the frequency from 32,768 Hz to 1 Hz. This accurate signal is then counted into units of seconds, minutes, and hours, and on request the stored information is processed by the decoders and display drivers to feed the four 7-segment LED displays. When the display is not in operation, special power-saving circuits on the chip reduce current consumption to only a few microcamps.

quartz crystal: "a disc or rod cut in the appropriate directions from a specimen of piezoelectric quartz, and accurately ground so that its natural resonance shall occur at a particular frequency"

LED (= light-emitting diode): "semi-conductor diode which radiates in the visible region"

IC (= integrated circuit): "a circuit which is fabricated as an assembly of electronic elements in a single structure, which cannot be subdivided without destroying its intended function"

divider: "circuit which reduces by an integral factor the number of pulses or alternations per second passing through it by suppressing the unwanted ones"

chip: "a small section of single crystal semi-conductor forming the substrate for an integrated circuit"

Text- und Transferfragen

The end of the assembly line?

Have you ever seen an assembly line? (If yes, where? Can you tell us something about it?)

Have you ever worked on such a line?

What do you think about assembly line work? How could it be made easier for the workers?

Can you tell us something about Volvo's experiment?

What is General Motors' answer to the problem of assembly line work?

Which solution do you think is the best?

What do you think about shift work?

Have you ever worked shifts? (*Oder:* Would you like to work shifts?)

What do you think about night work?

Do you think our industry could exist without shift and night work?

Do women get equal pay in Germany?

What's new on the market?

What does the English company offer?

What is the watch powered by?

What are "LEDs"?

What tools do you need to assemble the kit?

Have you ever done any soldering work?

What is an "IC"?

Do you think you could assemble such a watch?

Methodische Hinweise und Schlüssel

1 a. How long has she been living in Hamburg? – For six years, I think. **b.** How long has she been in the workshop? – For two or three hours, I think. **c.** How long have they been waiting in the office? – For an hour or so, I think. **d.** How long has she been translating letters? – Since eight o'clock this morning, I think.

2 a. unless **b.** In spite of **c.** although **d.** whereas **e.** unless

3 a. Since 1970 more and more electric furnaces have been constructed. **b.** Since 1970 more and more kits have been sold to do-it-yourselfers. **c.** Since 1970 more and more watches have been equipped with integrated circuits. **d.** Since 1970 more and more cars have been designed with the help of computers. **e.** Since 1970 more and more pocket calculators have been sold. **f.** Since 1970 more and more nuclear power stations have been built. **g.** Since 1970 more and more computers have been installed.

4 Dies ist die letzte schriftliche Kommunikationsübung und kann wieder als Hausaufgabe vorgesehen werden.

5 Freie Kommunikationsübung, daher ohne Schlüssel.

6 Wie Übung 5.

7 a. Have you ever worked on an assembly line? **b.** Yes, when I was in America. **c.** When was that? **d.** Four or five years ago, I think. **e.** Did you work in an automobile plant (*US; Br.:* car factory)? **f.** Yes, in Detroit.

g. What do you think about assembly line work? **h.** Well, assembly line work isn't very nice, of course, but I don't know if we can do without it. **i.** But in future, there will perhaps be better working methods. **j.** That's possible. We should, of course, do everything to make work more pleasent.

8 a. by . . . in **b.** by

TEST C

Test C, der Abschlußtest, umfaßt 82 Multiple-Choice-Items und einen schriftlichen Teil ("Writing a short article").

Abgetestet werden die Teilbereiche *Reading Comprehension, Structures and Vocabulary, Listening Comprehension, Prepositions, Stress, Word Order, Written Production*.

Schema zur Beurteilung des Teilbereichs *Written Production* ("Writing a short article"):

Beantwortung der 8 Leitpunkte (1: Safety belts? Air bags?
    2: Design of the car? 3: Training of the driver?
    4: Will traffic regulations help? 5: What about better roads?
    6: More autobahns? 7: More policemen? 8: What can the
   government do?)   **je Leitpunkt 3 Punkte**

Bewertungskriterien:

keine oder eine völlig unzureichende Antwort: 0 Punkte
zufriedenstellende Antwort mit Fehlern: 1 Punkt
zufriedenstellende Antwort ohne nennenswerte Fehler: 2 Punkte
gute Antwort ohne oder mit ganz geringfügigen Fehlern:
   3 Punkte

Wortschatz (umfangreicher Wortschatz – ausreichender
Wortschatz – geringer Wortschatz) . . . . **0–6 Punkte**

Rechtschreibung (kaum Fehler – einige Fehler – zahlreiche
Fehler) . . . . **0–5 Punkte**

                      = höchstens   **35 Punkte**

              + Multiple-Choice-Items   **82 Punkte**

                      = höchstens **117 Punkte**

Von diesen 117 Punkten sollte der Kursteilnehmer wenigstens 65 erreichen, wenn man von einem Bestehen des Tests sprechen will.

Von einer Einteilung in Notensysteme wird aber ausdrücklich abgesehen, da die Unterrichtsgegebenheiten doch zu unterschiedlich sind.

Wenn eine Bewertung irgendwelcher Art erforderlich sein sollte, so kann der Kursleiter sie leicht selbst vornehmen.

Bei Erwachsenen empfiehlt es sich sonst, nur die erreichte Punktzahl anzugeben, z. B. 95/117, 113/117 usw. (= 95 Punkte erreicht aus 117 möglichen usw.).

Schlüssel und Anmerkungen

1 right **2** right **3** wrong **4** right **5** right **6** wrong **7** wrong **8** wrong
9 right **10** wrong **11** right **12** wrong **13** wrong
14 all **15** All **16** Every **17** each **18** each
19a **20**a **21**b **22**a **23**b **24**d **25**b **26**c **27**b **28**b **29**a

(Listening Comprehension: Zuerst sollten den Kursteilnehmern einige Minuten Zeit zum Lesen der Fragen 30–36 gegeben werden. Dann wird der weiter unten folgende Text in normalem Sprechtempo vorgelesen. Danach folgt das zweite Vorlesen, diesmal aber mit kurzen Pausen – etwa eine Minute – zwischen den Abschnitten. Während des Vorlesens und in den dazwischenliegenden Pausen haben die Kursteilnehmer Gelegenheit, bei den Fragen 30–36 jeweils die richtige Lösung [a, b, c oder d] anzukreuzen:)

Energy for the future

Fuels like coal, gas and oil may no longer be available in the future. This fact, and rapidly rising costs, have created new interest in alternative sources of energy. If we could use the power of wind, water and sun, we would have enough energy for many, many years, and all of it pollution-free.
But is this really possible? What are the problems connected with these sources of power?

Water power

The use of water power is certainly not new. In the European countries, most of the existing possibilities of using rivers as power sources have already been developed, even in areas far away from big cities. Those that remain to be developed can only offer small benefits.

The tides have similarly attracted schemes over very many years. Only one tidal power station, however, has actually gone into full operation: It is in the North of France. There are plans for other tidal power stations in Europe, but many experts believe that such power stations will continue to play only a small role in meeting Europe's rising energy demands.

There is also the possibility of getting power from movement of waves. In Britain, for instance, a detailed study of several schemes of this sort is being made. An additional advantage of such power stations would be that the waves are at the same time reduced in height, thus creating an area of still water. Development time, however, seems rather long – around 15 years has been mentioned – and costs are likely to be high.

Wind power

As far as wind power is concerned, experts are more optimistic. Development times could be much shorter and costs much lower than with other schemes, they say. The costs will probably be in the range of from £150 to £200 per kilowatt, which is very much the same as with gas-, coal- or oil-fired power stations.

One of the people who believe in wind power is Professor Hütter of Stuttgart University. He designed a large machine of about 115 m diameter. Installed near the North German coast, such a machine could have a capacity of about three million watts and, he believes, could be built within three years. A 34 m diameter machine he designed some time ago ran successfully for over eight years and was only stopped when cheap oil killed interest in the use of wind power.

Solar power

Of all the schemes designed by experts, solar energy seems to be the most promising. Solar panels are being used and tested everywhere, and there are many areas in the world where solar power might turn out to be the cheapest form of energy. It will, however, be most successful as a form of direct heating and perhaps not so much as a source of electricity.

In a recent report, a group of experts said it was not true that Britain had not got enough sunshine. If only 3%0 of the land area of Britain, they said, was used for the collection of solar energy and the average efficiency was 30% (which could be achieved), they could collect all the energy they needed.

At the moment, Britain spends a lot less on solar energy research than, for instance, West Germany, Japan and the USA.

Does all this mean that we will be able to do without coal, gas and oil in the future? And what about nuclear power? Well, we will probably need all these sources of energy, each in its special field of application.

30c 31a 32a 33c 34c 35c 36a

(37) without (38) of (39) on (40) on to (41) of (42) in . . . of (43) from . . . of (44) to . . . of (45) into (46) from (47) on (48) on . . . through (49) of (49) of . . . to (50) like (51) to . . . of . . . on (52) in (53) on (54) into

55 ac | cu | mu | la | tor   56 co- | or | di | nates   57 in | ter | vals   58 in | ves | ti- | ga | tions   59 per | son | nel   60 sim | u | la | tion

61b **62**b **63**a **64**c **65**a **66**c **67**c **68**c **69**a **70**c **71**a **72**a **73**b **74**a **75**b

76 c e d b a / NASA scientists do a lot of research in the field of air safety. **77** b g f e c a d / The data will automatically produce drawings on a drafting machine. **78** b c a d / They use a computer for most of their calculations, thus saving a lot of time. **79** c b g d e a f / A lot of people will ask themselves: What good is the Star Trek gallery? **80** d b e a f g c / Since about 1960, NASA has been engaged in research to reduce jet noise. **81** e c a d b / He didn't know what to do when I told him that the machine had broken down. **82** c f a d b e / If she had known this, she would certainly have accepted the offer.

Writing a short article

Siehe Vorbemerkungen zu „TEST C".

Register